Introduction to the Theory
of Heinrich Schenker

Longman Music Series

Series Editor: Gerald Warfield

Introduction to the Theory of Heinrich Schenker

(Einführung in Die Lehre Heinrich Schenkers)

The Nature of the Musical Work of Art

Oswald Jonas

Translated and Edited by John Rothgeb

Longman
New York & London

Introduction to the Theory of Heinrich Schenker
The Nature of the Musical Work of Art

Longman Inc., 19 West 44th Street, New York, N.Y. 10036
Associated companies, branches, and representatives throughout the world.

Developmental Editor: Gordon T. R. Anderson
Editorial and Design Supervisor: Joan Matthews
Manufacturing and Production Supervisor: Anne Musso
Composition: Kingsport Press
Printing and Binding: The Murray Printing Company

Library of Congress Cataloging in Publication Data

Jonas, Oswald.
   [Einführung in die Lehre Heinrich Schenkers.
English]
   Introduction to the theory of Heinrich Schenker.

   (Longman music series)
   Translation of: Einführung in die Lehre Heinrich
   Schenkers, originally published in 1934 as: Das
   Wesen des musikalischen Kunstwerks.
   Includes index.
   1. Music—Analysis, appreciation.   2. Harmony.
3. Schenker, Heinrich, 1868–1935.   I. Rothgeb, John.
II. Title.   III. Series.
MT6.J76W43.   780′.1′5   81–8270
ISBN 0–582–28227–6   AACR2

Manufactured in the United States of America
9 8 7 6 5 4 3 2 1

Oswald Jonas (1897–1978)

Oswald Jonas's earliest memories were of himself entertaining his ten older sisters by singing entire operas to them. The scene is believable to those who knew him later: a prodigious musical memory coupled with a spontaneous, undiminishing zest for music making remained with him throughout his life. He considered himself a *musician*, scorning the term "musicologist." His ever-present humor—often barbed, often bawdy—masked a profound, philosophical concern with fundamental values; his passionately held convictions, his intolerance for pomposity in any form, earned him enemies as well as friends and disciples. Although severely critical of musical performances, a single perfectly articulated phrase could disarm him completely. It was to his students—often in individual lessons—that he most readily revealed his deepest musical insights. His interests were wide: a rare understanding and love for the visual arts were brought to a surprised public's attention when he lectured on American art collections during his first visits to Europe following World War II. An equally great understanding for poetry found expression in his illuminating work on the German art-song.

Oswald Jonas was born in Vienna on January 10, 1897. Although always preoccupied with music, he read law at the University of Vienna, receiving a Dr.jur. degree in 1921. He studied music privately with the well-known pianist Moriz

Violin, a close friend of Heinrich Schenker. Soon after their meeting, Schenker accepted him as his student and they worked together intensively for six years— mostly in the form of piano lessons, Schenker's preferred means of passing on his musical ideas. It was during this same period that Jonas became a devoted admirer of Karl Kraus, the great Viennese social critic and satirist, whose ideas, however, were incompatible with the highly conservative, German-national opinions of Schenker.

In 1930 Jonas left Vienna for Berlin, then musically and intellectually at its height. He was soon teaching privately and at the Stern Conservatory as well as working on his book, to be published in 1934 as *Das Wesen des Musikalischen Kunstwerks*. Its publication was received with the greatest enthusiasm by Schenker, who was delighted with this lucid introduction into his own theories. It also brought him the life-long friendship of Wilhelm Furtwängler, who had been profoundly influenced by Schenker's monograph on Beethoven's *Ninth Symphony*, and who later wrote about Jonas that "he possesses the rare gift of making difficult things clear and easily understandable." On returning to Vienna in 1935, Jonas founded the *Schenker Institut*, and together with Felix Salzer, he began publishing the periodical *Der Dreiklang*. Devoted to Schenker's theories, this important journal was unfortunately short-lived as Jonas immediately left the country upon the Nazi Anschluss of Austria in 1938. Schenker's works were, of course, banned during the Hitler years as he was of Jewish origin.

After an initial stay in England, Jonas emigrated to the United States. First teaching at the Longy School of Music in Boston, he later settled in Chicago, following an invitation to teach at the YMCA College. He was among the faculty that eventually founded Roosevelt College, now Roosevelt University, and he remained there as professor until retiring in 1962. The following three years were spent in Europe, which he had visited annually since 1950 and where he now lectured and held courses at various universities. Continuing his research in libraries—always a vital part of his work—as his interest focused more and more on the study of manuscripts, he also acquired an outstanding library of early editions and of slides and microfilms, which he used to illustrate his lectures. He contributed articles to a wide variety of music journals in English and German and he was an active editor. Besides preparing many of Schenker's works for republication, he made major contributions to the new Urtext editions of Bach, C.P.E. Bach, and Haydn among others.

Invited to be Regent's Professor at the University of California at Riverside in 1965, Jonas was to find a new home; he spent the rest of his life there, teaching at the university and continuing his regular trips to Europe. On one of the visits to Vienna he acquired the complete diaries of Schenker as well as much correspondence and manuscripts, published and unpublished, from his old friend, and first student, Erwin Ratz. This collection, now housed at the U.C.R. Library as part of the Oswald Jonas Memorial Collection, and that of Ernst Oster at the New York Public Library form the bulk of the extant Schenker Nachlass.

Oswald Jonas married Edith Schreier, who like him had emigrated from Vienna, in 1942. Until her death in 1974 their home was an unforgettably hospitable meeting place for colleagues, students, and friends from around the world. He died in Riverside on March 19, 1978.

Irene Schreier Scott
Oxford, England, 1981

Contents

Foreword to the English Edition

This introduction to Heinrich Schenker's theory was first published in 1934 by Saturn-Verlag, Vienna, as *Das Wesen des musikalischen Kunstwerks: Eine Einführung in die Lehre Heinrich Schenkers.* A second edition, revised by the author and with the original title and subtitle transposed, was published by Universal Edition, Vienna, in 1972. For the second edition, the German prose was revised to some extent, a few footnotes were added (including some references to Schenker's *Der freie Satz,*[1] which had not yet been published at the time of the first edition), and certain passages were deleted.[2]

Since the revisions for the 1972 edition were by the author himself, they should be considered definitive. Accordingly, the present translation is based chiefly on the later edition. In one instance, however, a portion of the original text has been restored. Example 97b (originally example 106) and the accompanying discussion by the author himself are especially striking. Although they do cause a slight interruption of continuity—evidently the reason for their omission from the second edition—, their intrinsic value is thought to justify their reinstatement.

When *Das Wesen des musikalischen Kunstwerks* was written, the author would have been familiar with all of Schenker's previous work, including most importantly the *Harmonielehre,* the monograph on Beethoven's Ninth Symphony, the complete run of *Der Tonwille* and its continuation in the three *Jahrbücher,* and the *Erläuterungsausgaben* of Beethoven's Sonatas opp. 101, 109, 110, and 111.[3] As he did not have access to Schenker's final and definitive work, *Der freie Satz,* the fidelity and perspicuity with which he was able to present the main outlines of Schenker's theory are remarkable. The focus, appropriately, is on Schenker's central concept of *composing-out (Auskomponierung)*[4] and the spe-

---

1. Translated, by Ernst Oster, as *Free Composition.* See appendix D, Works of Heinrich Schenker.

2. Much of the deleted material consisted of quotations from Schenker's earlier works; it is probable that after more than three decades the author regarded some of those explanations as superseded by Schenker's later work.

3. See appendix D, Works of Heinrich Schenker.

4. An important related term is *Prolongation,* which in Schenker's writing is often synonymous with *Auskomponierung,* but is used also in expressions such as *Prolongationen der Gesetze der Stimmführung* (extended or modified applications of the laws of voice leading).

cific techniques by which it is executed. The treatment of strict counterpoint—of its fundamental formations and their status as controlling prototypes in free composition—is particularly valuable. There is little detailed discussion of Schenker's theory of strata *(Schichten)*, and no rigorous characterization of the three broad categories of foreground, middleground, and background strata. It could not have been otherwise, for the dividing lines between these categories were drawn (at least in part) by Schenker himself only in *Der freie Satz*.

Chapter 1, Music and Nature, is concerned with certain prerequisites of art in general and the way they are manifested in music in particular. The account of the origin of the major and minor systems, and the reasons behind their particular course of development, follows rather closely that given by Schenker in *Harmony*, except that certain superfluities (the "mysterious" nature of the number 5, for example) have been trimmed away. Schenker did not revise his view of the tonal system in his later writings, and we may assume that he would have regarded Jonas's account as definitive.

Chapter 2 begins the first systematic presentation of composing-out with the most basic technique of all: arpeggiation. The last section introduces the concept of the passing tone, which leads directly to the considerations in chapter 3.

In a sense the heart of the book, chapter 3 shows how the Schenkerian notion of linear progression follows directly from certain considered observations of the elementary voice-leading formations of strict counterpoint. Section 2g, The Conjunction and Alignment of Linear Progressions, and section 4, The Occurrence of Dissonance in a Consonant State, are of critical significance for Schenkerian theory.

Although extremely valuable in themselves, the first two sections of chapter 4 are less definitive when compared with the final formulation of Schenker's ideas in *Der freie Satz*. Because the latter is now available in translation, I have not annotated these sections extensively.

Oswald Jonas was himself a highly original thinker about music, as is evident from certain passages of the book that present ideas for which he was not particularly indebted to Schenker, such as the discussions of rhythm (chapter 1, section 3) and of sonata and rondo forms (chapter 4, section 3). Above all, appendix A should be cited in this connection for its lucid and perceptive treatment of the relation of word and tone. The art song occupied a central place in Jonas's musical life and work; his involvement with the song literature was of a thoroughly practical nature, for he coached innumerable classes in the performance of songs (chiefly German and French) over a span of several decades in both Europe and America.

Like Schenker, Jonas was more than just a theorist: he was a philosopher of language—specifically, the language of music. And as radically different as his politics were from Schenker's—he found Schenker's notion of German supremacy particularly rebarbative—the two men were in almost perfect agreement on all matters directly related to music. Therefore, even when Jonas deals with issues that Schenker did not address extensively, his ideas are thoroughly compatible with Schenkerian thinking.

I have added many explanatory footnotes and occasional brief amplifications within the text itself. All footnotes and textual interpolations set off by square brackets [ ] are my own unless otherwise indicated. Cross references, as well as references to works by Schenker and Jonas, have been added, but I have not attempted the formidable task of citing relevant sources within the extensive secondary literature.

The interpretative examples fall into two categories. Most numerous are those intended to reveal particular motivic or local contrapuntal features. A few examples approach Schenkerian voice-leading graphs *(Urlinientafeln)* of complete works or relatively long or self-contained sections of works. These graphs are sometimes incompletely interpreted; in particular, the bass is often merely sketched without full indication of the varying weight and significance of the bass tones: there is often no notational differentiation, for example, between passing tones and tones that stand for scale degrees *(Stufen)*. Certain graphic symbols, such as braces and brackets, have been tacitly added for clarification; notification is provided in footnotes of any significant additions of my own.

Two of the examples appeared to warrant more extensive amplification, either by the inclusion of a larger context or by additional interpretation. This I have provided in my appendix C, supplementary Examples.

Schenker's work has been represented and interpreted abundantly in books and periodicals during the past half-century. Normally one can only speculate about how Schenker himself would have regarded such efforts; but in the case of *Das Wesen des musikalischen Kunstwerks* we happen to possess an exceptional piece of evidence concerning its reception by Schenker. In the summer of 1934, while vacationing in the Tyrol, Schenker presented a copy of the book to his wife, who was also a musician and his amanuensis for many years. A facsimile of Schenker's inscription in that copy (which eventually found its way into Jonas's library) is shown in plate 1.

Plate 1.

The transcription reads:

> Meinem theueren LieLiechen,
> der Grossmama dieses Enkel=
> buches
>
>   Grossvater Heinrich
> Mitte Juli 1934
> Böckstein
>
> (To my dear LieLie,
> grandmother of this grandchild-
> book
>
>   Grandfather Heinrich
> Mid-July 1934
> Böckstein)

My heartfelt thanks go to Professor Jurgen Thym of the Eastman School of Music and to Mrs. Irene Schreier Scott, both of whom painstakingly read the manuscript and made many indispensable suggestions. Mrs. Scott kindly made available the facsimile for plate no. 1.

To the author's wish, expressed in chapter 4, section 2, that this volume might motivate further study of Schenker's work, I should like to add my own that the translation may in addition provide an incentive for study of the other writings of Oswald Jonas, outstanding musician and scholar.

John Rothgeb
Binghamton, N.Y.

Preface to the Second Edition

A new edition of a book that first appeared thirty years ago poses special problems. The purpose of the new edition can no longer be the same as that of the original one. In the interim, Schenker's theory has become widely disseminated, and the resistance that it originally met has softened to some extent; but at the same time, the ever greater need to render the theory understandable and useful has brought with it the need for a more general introduction.

The criteria for such an introduction have changed, moreover, because Schenker's principal work, *Der freie Satz*, was published posthumously in 1935—the year of his death, and a year after the first edition of this book. *Der freie Satz* represents a synopsis of his theory, in a sense its codification; but in many respects, to understand it one must be familiar with the works that preceded. Our "introduction" will endeavor to ease this difficulty, which is compounded by the fact that many of the earlier works are out of print and thus not readily obtainable.

Much has been changed and, it is hoped, improved in the new edition; but at the same time an effort was made to preserve the book insofar as possible in its original form, in which it won Schenker's approval and highest praise, even at the risk that one or another of its formulations might appear to be superseded. If the book proves serviceable as a "stepping stone" toward the arduous study of *Der freie Satz*, it will in any case have accomplished its mission and justified its republication.

Preface to the First Edition

Those who fail to see how truth facilitates practice may be pleased to denigrate and ridicule, just to make an excuse, to a certain extent, for their own ill-conceived and tedious activity.

Goethe

Works of art are not created by feeling; thus feeling does not suffice for understanding them.

Konrad Fiedler

The work of Heinrich Schenker has long stood in need of an introduction to serve as an aid to the reader. Unfortunately it cannot be denied that Schenker's writings, which provide access to the musical work of art in a unique way, have met with little understanding. This is all the more regrettable because in those writings, perhaps for the first time, theory is undertaken not for its own sake, but in an intimate connection with art—indeed, with art in its highest maturity and perfection. The interpretation of works of musical genius and mystery: that is what the artist Heinrich Schenker offers us. *Neue musikalische Theorien und Phantasien, von einem Künstler*[1] was the title under which Schenker's first major work, *Harmonielehre*, appeared. With the pseudonym "an artist," he deliberately set himself apart at the outset from other theorists.

Because Schenker's theory is closely bound to art, it imposes demands of a sort completely different from the usual ones. Besides motivation and a love of art, the student must be possessed of both a sensibility capable of subtle discrimination, and the capacity for self denial that is always needed for any consideration of fundamental problems. The finished work of art conceals within itself countless assumptions—imponderables that demand of those who would re-create with understanding (and every higher act of comprehension is re-creation) a commensurate expenditure of effort. They demand an accomplishment at least worthy of the deed of the genius.

Besides this difficulty, Schenker's work presents another one of a special kind. His theory itself, naturally, has undergone its own development, which extends over twenty years and more. It could not have been otherwise, because the theory

[1. *New Musical Theories and Fantasies, by an Artist.* See appendix D, Works of Heinrich Schenker.]

is not an intellectually manufactured system made to fit certain initial assumptions, but is derived rather from intimate knowledge of the masterworks. For this, however, an untold amount of experience was required, and a constant expansion of the capacity for artistic hearing. Incidentally, this fact alone, which shows Schenker as a thoroughly practical artist, should give pause to those critics who accuse him of theoretical hairsplitting. Up to now, Schenker's work has encountered no serious—that is to say, well-grounded—refutation. The proud motto [of Kant's] that Schenker placed at the head of his first *Jahrbuch*,[2] "There is no danger here of being refuted, only of being misunderstood," still applies. And it is not without significance that Schenker prefaces that publication, which may be considered the beginning of his principal work, with a quotation from Kant. In 1773 Kant wrote to Marcus Herz:

> You will look diligently but in vain in the Fair catalog for a certain name among the K's. After all of my hard work, nothing would have been easier for me than to parade that name in the catalog with not inconsiderable works that I have nearly finished. But I have made such good progress toward my goal of reforming a discipline that has long occupied the attention of half the philosopical world that I now see myself in possession of *a theoretical concept that completely resolves the former puzzle* and brings the operation of reason, free from factors external to it, under rules that are secure and easy of application. Therefore I hold stubbornly to my original intention not to be distracted by the seductions of authorship and seek fame in a more popular field before I have smoothed my thorniest and rockiest soil and made it free for general cultivation.

But Schenker, because of the nature of his material, was unable to work in this way. His publications present his concepts at any given moment as they had developed through experience. His *theoretical concept*, the *Ursatz* (fundamental structure), likewise undergoes a process of evolution through the series of works. And he established his terminology (first the term *"Urlinie"* [fundamental line]) before he himself was able to arrive at a completely clear formulation of the concept. This caused severe misunderstanding and posed the difficulty mentioned above for those seeking access to his ideas.

Perhaps the present work may serve as a temporary remedy, one that is all the more urgently needed because Schenker's first publication, *Harmonielehre*, which is in many respects a prerequisite to the understanding of his work, has long been out of print. The publication in the foreseeable future of the final volume, *Der freie Satz*, will provide definite clarity and systematic organization.

Finally I should add that in quoting from *Harmonielehre*—which, because of its unavailability, happened quite frequently—I was guided by two principles. First, to put explanations of its examples into the form that emerged from the later works and the evolution of Schenker's theory. And second, I was particularly concerned to show how already in *Harmonielehre*—published in 1906—we often find in embryonic form ideas that were fully developed only later.

[2. See appendix D, Works of Heinrich Schenker.]

List of Abbreviations
Used in the Examples

c.f.	cantus firmus
chrom.	chromatic (note)
cpt.	counterpoint
n.n.	neighboring note
prg.	(linear) progression, preceded by size of interval spanned, e.g., 3-prg. (third-progression)
sim.	simile
st.	strophe

Chapter 1

Music and Nature

Section 1. The Act of Association

> The most dreamlike and, one might say, "created" of the arts—the one
> that, among all arts, caused the severest birth pangs and therefore the
> one that was bequeathed to us last of all—the youngest of the arts,
> music, is lost!
>
> Schenker, *Kontrapunkt I*

Every work of art requires an act of association. As expression of a specific
conceptual realm, it needs to communicate by some means intrinsic to its raw
material if it is to make contact with the recipient's power of comprehension. A
work in an alien or invented language, which, because it does not owe its origin
to any such generally valid principle, fails to arouse vivid images in the hearer
or viewer, is dead.

Certain ideas are inseparably bound to the poet's material, to each word of
his language; with their help he is able to make clear his intentions and his formations *(Gestaltungen)*. And just as the original, most primitive impulse toward
artistic creativity finds its expression in imitation, so the first response on the
part of the recipient is the joy of recognition.[1] Whether we stop here or advance
to true artistic creation as well as artistic comprehension, the prerequisite remains
association—that is, the connection of the material to specific ideas.

The poet finds in language, and the visual artist in the world of figures that
surrounds both him and us, the raw material upon which his art imposes shape.

[1. "The ever stronger inner desire of music to follow its own course, to strive toward
expansion of content, found its counterpart in the pleasure the ear derived from repetition—
a joy in recognition itself" (Schenker, *Free Composition*, p. 99).]

1

In other cases the initial ideas are purpose-related, like those that guide the architect; necessities that reside in nature and therefore (because they are sensed equally by all of us) have general validity, such as observance of the law of gravity or rhythmic requirements, enter only later. Perhaps one could distinguish between direct and indirect associations—associations like those in language and the spatial world that evoke immediate images, on the one hand, and those that gain their contact with nature by way of forces dormant in all of us, on the other. How does this apply in music?

Lacking any association with the outer, spatial world, lacking purpose, the tone conjures up only the tone itself. The purely emotional reactions it evokes in the individual are of so vague a nature and yet so varied that cause and effect could never be unequivocally related to one another. A conscious creative process *(Gestaltung)* could not be based on this. Thus music, in its earliest stages, before it had achieved independence, had to subordinate itself to other forms of expression in order to exist at all. Music, whether associated with word or merely with rhythm, remained accompanimental: religious ritual, the song, and the dance where always in the foreground. (We shall return later to the special role that music, because of its lack of direct association, assigns to rhythm.) It was the lack of direct association with Nature that delayed the development of music as an independent art for such a long time. When poetry and visual art had already reached their highest maturity, music remained in its infancy. Now if comprehensibility on the one hand and imitation as a first stimulus to formal organization on the other are both founded on association (and therefore on repetition), music was obliged to provide this repetition from within, since none was available from outside. It should perhaps be remarked that the occasional imitation in music of sounds from nature such as bird song or the murmur of running water or the forest has nothing to do with its lack of external association. Leaving aside the fact that these are merely isolated cases, they count only as secondary features of a poetical character, similar to the use by language of onomatopoeic associations simultaneously with its unambiguous verbal associations. (Schenker calls such suggestions from nature associations of second hand [*Assoziationen aus zweiter Hand*], external associations.) The principle of repetition in music, then, grew out of the urge to imitate, which provided the first means of mastering the raw material. The early epoch of musical development is rife with the technique of imitation, the first attempts at shaping musical form and content. To be sure, it was still a great distance from here to the eventual forging of the motive, music's analog to the word; and other basic experiments had to be carried out along the way. Nevertheless, with the principle of repetition the first approach to artistic expression was provided, and the first avenue of communication with the listener prepared. "Only by repetition can a series of tones be given a specific identity and a specific purpose. Repetition therefore serves the same purpose to the original tone-succession as associations with nature serve the creations of other art forms."[2]

---

2. Schenker, *Harmonielehre*, p. 5. [My translation differs from the one given in *Harmony*, p. 5.]

Section 2.   Repetition as a Device of Art

Once the artist had recognized the significance of the necessity for repetition, a previously undetected possibility for variegated construction was made available to him. It was natural for the artist to take pleasure in *forming* his repetitions, in giving them a different external appearance and masking their clarity—in saying the same thing, but in a way not immediately recognizable by the ear. Moreover, because the expectation of repetition was an initial premise, the repetition could be delayed and tension thereby generated. In the case of multiple repetitions, variation even became an imperative for artistic diversity, and thus a fertile field was presented for cultivation by the artist's creative powers. Associations function not only with respect to the small motive but also over the long span, where they help to shape the form of a work and to bind it together securely.

In considering the following examples, we focus our attention first of all only on the principle of repetition *per se;* discussion of the prerequisites for actual composing will follow later. By the same token, we can make only passing reference here to those concealed traits that so miraculously guarantee coherence in the masterworks. To begin with, then, a few simple examples of motivic repetition:

Example 1.   Beethoven, Sonata in F Major, op. 10 no. 2

Example 2.   Beethoven, Sonata in G Major, op. 14 no. 2

The following examples may be more difficult for the listener to follow:

Example 3.   Mozart, Sonata in C Major, K. 545

bars 3–4   bars 5–8

b)

The enlarged repetition in bars 5–8 *(a–g–f–e)* is brought out by the retention, throughout its course, of the same type of passage-work; Mozart changes this pattern only at bar 9 where the tone *d*, a new element, arrives. Here it is appropriate to call attention to the close interaction between surface configuration and the forces at work in the background. ("There is nothing in the skin that is not in the bones."—Goethe.)

Example 4. Beethoven, Sonata in E Minor, op. 90

The sketch reveals Beethoven's superbly enlarged variation of the second repetition. The variation was doubly necessary, since a mechanical continuation by an exact transposition, approaching *b* through the passing tone *c♯* instead of *c♮* in bar 10, would have led to *D* major.

Example 5. Mozart, Fantasy in D Minor, K. 397

In example 5, an insignificant ornament gains meaning by planting the seed of the continuation [see the brackets].

Example 6. Beethoven, Sonata in A♭ Major, op. 110

Here too, an [apparently] insignificant ornament is given life by being entrusted with the task of repeating what preceded.

Sometimes the demand for repetition can influence the overall plan of a whole composition and lend it a truly poetic-programmatic content. Thus Mozart's *d-*

minor Fantasy has as an introduction a free improvisation with arpeggiations, apparently without relation to what is to come:

Example 7.   Mozart, Fantasy in D Minor, K. 397

Yet these bars become the motto that determines the course of the entire work.

Example 8.   Mozart, Fantasy

In a highly artistic melodic unfolding, the Adagio attempts to repeat. (Note especially the retained articulation into pairs of bars!) [Compare examples 8b and 7b.] But the repetition breaks off in bars 7–8. Because of the series of half steps set in motion by the neighboring tone in bar 5, Mozart arrives only at *e* over the dominant in bar 8 instead of moving through *eb* to *c♯*. Now there begins a searching and probing until at last—what a marvel of conception and goal-directed construction!—at the *tempo primo* [bar 45], another repetition occurs, this time in a form that is faithful to the introduction. The newly rediscovered *eb* even receives a cadenza-like elaboration!

Example 9.   Mozart, Fantasy

Another specific way of achieving musical cohesion, known as "linkage technique," is also based on the principle of repetition. Linkage technique means that a new phrase takes as its initial idea the end of the immediately preceding one and then continues independently, either within the same formal unit:

Example 10.   Beethoven, Sonata in G Major, op. 49 no. 2

or to initiate a new section (in this case, the Trio):

Example 11.   Brahms, Clarinet Sonata, op. 120 no. 1, Third Movement

In example 12, several transitory bars are used in a new way.

Example 12.   Schubert, Symphony no. 9 in C Major

(Compare Brahms, Violin Sonata op. 108, last movement, bars 37ff.) Another form of linkage technique consists in initiating a repetition that will either be completed in (example 13) or in part postponed until (example 14) the following formal unit. Brahms was particularly fond of this type of linkage.

Example 13.   Chopin, Nocturne in F Major, op. 15 no. 1

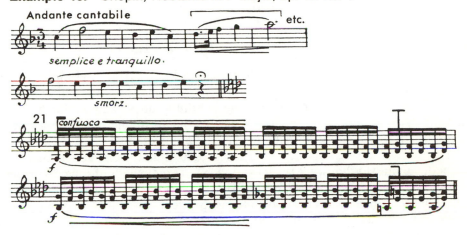

Example 14.   Brahms, Horn Trio, op. 40, Last Movement

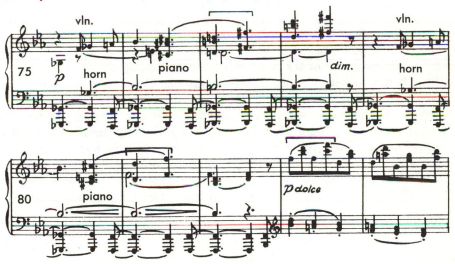

More will be said later about this and other possibilities as well. The extraordinarily brilliant construction of the rondo form in the final movement of the Violoncello Sonata in *F*, op. 99, also rests on this inspired technique for achieving coherence. (Further examples will be cited in chapter 4.)

Yet it must be repeated that these majestic spans and arches with which the artist learned to establish coherence within his work would never have been possi-

ble without the basic prerequisites to be treated in section 4: those cryptic man-
dates, that *unique—and therefore irrevocably binding—hint* that Nature has
inscribed into the human ear. How could the works of man attain such perfection
without the help of nature? How could style and high art ever have developed
from "simple imitation"?

Before pursuing these matters further, we address a phenomenon of special
importance for the principle of repetition and for music in particular.

Section 3.   The Significance of Rhythm in Music

There are probably few concepts so badly abused as that of rhythm.[3] The most
superficial discussions, be they in one art or another, always tell us about the
large rhythms, the rhythmic energy, the rhythmic lines, and so forth. This is
especially true in music: rhythmic interpretations form the sum and substance
of most analyses, usually without any explanation of how they were derived.
Indeed, it often appears as though rhythm and music were synonymous, and
judgments about rhythm were the most important component of musical criticism.
But the obvious consideration that rhythmic processes, because they are of a
general nature, are at bottom completely independent of tonal conceptions[4] should
make us suspicious of such an attitude. There are rhythmic processes that we
perceive optically, and others that we perceive aurally—processes that occur in
space and others that occur in time. Our sensitivity to them is innate—physiologi-
cally grounded, in a sense. If we were to isolate the essential element common
to all processes that we perceive and describe as rhythmic, it would have to be
regularity of recurrence—repetition at equal time intervals. This consistent recurrence awakens in us a feeling of security; the future course of events appears
ensured by the regularity of the past. Moreover, processes which by their nature
would be difficult to perceive clearly—for example, because they occupy large
spaces or long spans of time—become, through subdivision into equal parts, more
orderly, more distinct—in a word, *comprehensible*. Because rhythm, first of all,
aims only at an initial organization of our conceptions, it counts as one of the
basic requirements of our intellect and our perceptual mechanisms; therefore it
is not bound to any particular material, and it cannot constitute the unique requirement of any one art form. Rather, it is just one of the prerequisites upon which
human creativity *in general* depends. Only when this is clear can we proceed

---

[3. *Rhythmus*. The meaning in German, as in the Greek *rhythmos*, includes the notion
of regularity of temporal organization. "Rhythm," which often connotes variability projected onto a background of regularity (meter), is therefore not an exact equivalent. Indeed,
the meaning of *Rhythmus* as it is used in this section often comes close to meter, but it
is more comprehensive. Where "rhythm" is used in the translation it should be understood
as referring to temporal organization in a general way but with particular emphasis upon
aspects that manifest regularity.]

[4. Here especially the emphasis is upon regular aspects of rhythm. Jonas's argument
in the following paragraphs is that specifically musical rhythm, with its usual connotation
of variability, is precisely *dependent* upon tonal processes.]

without danger to investigate why the rhythmic element nevertheless stands more in the foreground in one art form than in another.

Clearly, this is related to the specific character of the material. The less comprehensible the material is by nature, that is, the fewer possibilities it offers for association with the external world, the more welcome and necessary the organizing principle of rhythm will be. It is upon the character of the material in this respect that the often cited kinship of music and architecture rests. But however much rhythmic organization—manifested in architecture as symmetry—facilitates the perceptual comprehension of a building, it has little to do with the actual artistic idea of architecture. Otherwise, wouldn't a counterfeit architecture, one that sought to make its strongest effect through emphasis on the rhythmic element, also make an artistic impression? If music (as we have seen) in its beginnings had to seek out and shape its own repetitions, what was more natural than to take refuge in the repetitions provided by rhythm—to take rhythm as an initial impetus? Primitive man, by the same token, can approach music only by way of rhythm, for rhythm, which is latent in him as in everyone, provides his only access to music.

However, as music's repetitions acquired in the course of events their particular shape and form, simple rhythm necessarily proved insufficient in the long run. The very requirement of regularity, essential to rhythm, worked at cross purposes with the demand for variety intrinsic to art; strict regularity of succession would soon lead to paralysis and monotony without any trace of expression. But artistic creation, to be sure, would be impossible without the backing of an organizing principle of regularity—a principle that, by providing orientation, allowed us to become conscious of diversity. Therefore our critique will focus on the question of how far the artist succeeds in countering the purely impulsive instinct of rhythmic imitation. A danger can become a blessing if, correctly understood by the artist, it provides a stimulus for his creative process. The limits within which the artist must work here will again be those imposed by comprehensibility. This must be preserved through contact with nature (in our case, with the organizing principle [of regularity]). Clearly, then, it is entirely up to artistic formation and its resources to establish the correct balance between natural organization on the one side and artistic formation on the other. These resources, however, belong exclusively to the world of tone, from which alone they can be created. Our natural feeling for rhythm can only draw our attention to the polarity [between natural organization and artistic formation] by reacting to it, actually exercising control. Under such circumstances it can only be regarded as a ridiculous and childish presumption when, as has happened all too often in the past and still happens, theorists, pompously boasting of their own "sense of rhythm," find it necessary to correct those deviations [from regularity]—deviations whose essence is variety, as it is exhibited by the masterworks.[5] The masters did not succumb to the force of an instinctive feeling, but sought instead to lend it validity in a more intelligent and artistic way.

[5. This will be amplified in the paragraphs that follow.]

A simple example can show how tonal life is ravished by conventional theory to satisfy a rigid conception of rhythm:[6]

Example 15.   Beethoven, Sonata in E Minor, op. 90

Example 16.   Riemann, *Präludien und Studien I*, p. 94

In the Beethoven: inspired pursuit of tonal life; expansion of the sixteenth-note upbeat to eighth notes (thus the *portato* indication) to avoid breaking up the melodic flow—otherwise it would have to read as follows:

Example 16a.

—thereby also preparing the alteration of bar 3. Thus we find an *elimination* of exact rhythmic correspondence for the sake of the melodic line and the avoidance of monotony.

In the Riemann: rigid adherence to the eighth-note upbeat, even if the true sense and content is lost in the process. A small example, yet does it not reveal fully the unbridgeable chasm that separates a mere theorist from an artist? From this it is understandable why Riemann in his *System der Rhythmik* arrives at the false definition of *motive* as "the concrete content of a rhythmically basic time-unit."[7] This definition shows blatantly how concepts of tonal life are forced into rhythmic molds and even subordinated to them.

What confusion prevails in this area may be demonstrated by a sentence from a work by August Halm, a person of high artistic stature: "The superiority of rhythm [over the purely linear melodic element] does not appear so surprising when we consider that rhythm is not expressed exclusively in music, and is something that we expect as a matter of course."[8] Instead of concluding from the general character of the concept that a certain caution would be necessary in

6. Example 16 is from Hugo Riemann, *Präludien und Studien: Gesammelte Aufsätze zur Aesthetik, Theorie, und Geschichte der Musik* (3 vols.; Frankfurt am Main: Bechhold, 1895), I, p. 94.

[7. Hugo Riemann, *System der musikalischen Rhythmik und Metrik* (Leipzig: Breitkopf und Härtel, 1903), p. 18.]

8. August Halm, *Einführung in die Musik* [(Berlin: Deutsche Buch-Gemeinschaft, 1926), p. 91. The bracketed interpolation is by the author.].

using it in musical criticism, Halm arrives at the notion of "superiority"; what possible meaning can the word have here?

Yet another example: the theme from Mozart's *A*-Major Sonata, which Riemann has interpreted "rhythmically" on several different occasions.[9]

Example 17.   Mozart, Sonata in A Major, K. 331

Example 18.   Riemann, *Katechismus der Kompositionslehre II*, p. 17

Riemann is obviously disturbed here by the fact that the melodically leading principal tones do not fall on the strong beat of the measure. But it does not disturb him in the least that precisely this discrepancy, together with the need to avoid a second monotonous repetition, engenders the construction with enlargement [of the third $a^1-c\sharp^2$ in bars 3–4]; he stands by his initially posited rhythmic schema, which cuts this very enlargement in two. Obviously he has not even noticed it, to say nothing of having understood its meaning. (The true meaning of such a procedure will be discussed later[10] in connection with composing-out and the linear progressions of voice leading.) Riemann turns a living and varied organism into a caricature that has nothing to do with the content of the original. And for what reason? In the last analysis, only because the essentially more strongly emphasized apex tones in bars 1–2 fall on weak beats, which indeed anyone can hear, but which Mozart, of all people, is supposed not to have heard!

We have seen in the preceding pages how the artist stands in relation to natural forces—how, through artistic construction, he rises above mere imitation and achieves style. Our last example, and the "correction" that it had to suffer as the result of a "natural" interpretation, lead us to another special relationship between rhythmic organization and music. This involves the so-called "bar-line problem," which requires discussion [in the following paragraphs].

All acoustical processes unfold in time, and thus, by implication, music unfolds in time. But how do we really perceive time? Time passes; it seems long or short

---

[9. Example 18 is from Riemann, *Katechismus der Kompositionslehre* (2 vols.; Leipzig: Hesse's Verlag, 1889), II, p. 17.]

[10. See chap. 3, footnote 24; also *Free Composition* §290 and fig. 141.]

to us depending on whether or not it is filled with content. We can never say exactly how much time has passed. In other words, we do not perceive time directly: we can measure it only indirectly in relation to other happenings. An auxiliary means is needed to make us conscious of it. Thus in order to evaluate and measure temporal processes we require a simple measuring unit for time. With such a measuring unit we put time, which was formerly only abstract, into concrete terms. One could perhaps speak of a materialization of time by means of its subdivision. This subdivision takes place only through rhythm. Rhythm, therefore, represents a principle that operates upon time from without and divides it into perceptibly small segments, which then can be assessed and controlled in relation to one another on the basis of their equality of duration. Rhythm indirectly makes us conscious of time. This fact and necessity, however, have frequently led to the error of placing rhythm and processes that unfold through time into a direct correspondence.[11] It must be stressed again that rhythm represents a principle that is inborn in us, which operates in a completely general way, and which merely attains an elevated significance for temporal processes. It defines a particular span of time by dividing it into segments that we can easily identify. The regularity of these segments, which represents a fundamentally anti-artistic principle, indirectly becomes the strongest motivating force for shaping (Gestaltung). The first reaction [of art] is to establish a hierarchy in terms of light and heavy through emphasis—that is, the bar. The bar binds several time units together into a higher-level unit. These higher units, in turn, alternate in a regular way. They lead to the rhythm of groups of bars and, ultimately, to the unification of larger sections. It is the *simultaneous* operation and the interdependence of the two factors—regularity, which flows from the inborn sense of rhythm and finds its expression in the bar line, and, on the other side, the shaping of ideas with musical resources in such a way as to counteract monotony—which is mostly overlooked today.

The masters want to make us forget the bar line for the sake of higher-order connections; they take the greatest pains to shape their works with the maximum possible variety—and this they accomplish the more fully as their rhythmic sense keeps them oriented, controlling and, when necessary, even admonishing. For Mozart in example 17, the bar lines immediately present a source of inspiration. In sharp contrast to all of this we see the theorist with his stifling schema, which, through its insistence on invariable correspondence of bar lines and compositional stress, produces a tedious sameness. It is little wonder that the theorist, working on such a primitive basis, regards the masterworks as needing correction. With this kind of thinking, the author of the book *Rhythm and Performance* reaches the conclusion that a major portion of the classical masterworks (almost sixty per cent of Chopin's Nocturnes, etc.) are incorrectly notated. This conclusion, instead of thoroughly discrediting and reducing to absurdity the study that produced it, leads to further serious debate of the alleged inadequacies of notation and to the recommendation that editors undertake a "rectification." One might expect that such a discrepancy between masterwork and theory would teach us that the masters must have proceeded on completely different artistic assumptions;

[11. *Verbindung*, literally "connection." The error is illustrated by example 18.]

but instead, reality is distorted to fit a theory. And this, finally, is the lamentable "bar-line problem," whose very existence exposes the bleak state of our theory. (See examples 94 and 95 [and the accompanying discussion].)

The "bar-line problem" shows us the contrast between the masters who, conscious of means and ends, shape their works proudly and freely, and the helpless theorist who literally chases after the accents with his bar lines, rendering them meaningless in the process.[12] Doesn't the theorist's inability correspond exactly to the perception of primitive man, who identifies only the purely rhythmic organization in a succession of tones? For the theorist, tones are reduced to a mere means to an end, and rhythm is raised to the status of a primary goal!

It has often been objected against Schenker's analytical writings that they do not adequately address rhythmic aspects—in direct contrast to the conventional analyses, which for the most part are filled with nothing else. The foregoing exposition will help to explain this. We have ascribed to rhythm an influence on the tonal life that is, to be sure, effective, but nevertheless indirect. Schenker was concerned above all with the actual *tonal shape (Tongestalt)* and the description of the forces that contributed to its formation.

Section 4.   The Principle of Association Intrinsic to Music

Nature has, however, provided music with one—and only one—prototype. It took a long time for the artist to understand Nature's hint, and a still greater effort was required to render it fruitful for art. It is in the phenomenon of the overtone series that Nature has given us her hint. "This much-discussed phenomenon, which constitutes Nature's only source for music to draw upon, is much more familiar to the instinct of the artist than to his consciousness. The artist's practical action thus has a much deeper foundation than his theoretical understanding of it."[13] The sounding tone is not acoustically simple; rather, like light, it is a composite. It contains a whole series of tones that emanate from the fundamental and rise from simple relationships, which are clearly audible, through more distant and less audible ones, and finally enter imperceptible regions. The tone therefore has its own life, its own procreative instinct.

There are two important conclusions that we can derive from the presence of overtones. The first is that the notion of polyphony, of simultaneity, is contained in Nature, and is therefore, in a certain measure, intrinsic to the ear. Moreover, we can infer from the order in which the overtones appear and their respective strengths a standard of measurement of their qualities and degrees of relationship as Nature would have them judged. This is all the more significant because it provides us, for the first time, with a frame of reference for critical hearing.

---

12. We will see something similar later on in appendix A, The Relation of Word and Tone, in regard to the correspondence of bar line and poetic scansion.

[13. Schenker, *Harmony*, pp. 20–21.]

Assuming *C* as fundamental, the overtone series appears as in example 19.

Example 19.

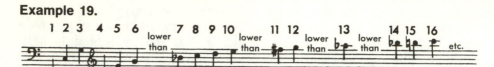

The [fundamental] tone produces the octave, which represents merely an identity expressed in a higher register; next the fifth, resulting from a ternary division; and the third, which corresponds to the number five. (The fourth partial naturally represents the second octave of the fundamental, which can be understood as the octave of the second partial.) Because the distances between tones become smaller as we ascend, the seventh partial is not identical to the [interval of the] seventh of our tonal system; the seventh, contrary to widespread opionion, is *not* based on the seventh partial in Nature. We observe also in this series that the fourth appears only as a relation between the third and fourth partials: it does not occur as an interval above the fundamental. This fact is one of highest significance, and its consequences will be examined in detail.

Because of the ear's tendency to prefer simpler relationships, where available, to more complicated ones, the ninth partial, for example, will manifest itself rather as the third partial of the third partial. This characteristic tendency of tones to appear as closer—and therefore stronger—overtones also has important consequences.

Now what should the artist's position be with regard to this natural phenomenon, the overtone series? Can he simply adopt it directly, as it is? We have already mentioned that the perceptibility of overtones decreases as their distance from the fundamental and the complexity of their relationship increase. Nature, with her phenomena, is incommensurable. The artist who wishes to make her forms usable is forced to simplify them. Again, it is comprehensibility that has to serve as the artist's guide. The artist hearkens to the prescription of Nature; but no one could follow that prescription in its entirety, and it would not occur to a true artist to try. Even the most faithful imitation could not incorporate Nature's causality.

In limiting their resources to the strongest overtones with the simplest relationships (two, three, and five), composers have simply used the law of abbreviation, which is absolutely necessary [in Art]. The strongest partials in the overtone series are those shown in example 20, which represent nothing but the triad.

Example 20.

The triad thus reveals itself as a requirement of Nature and, at the same time, of Art. The essence of artistic activity, which consists in clearly motivated construction along with fulfillment of Nature's postulate, entails that Art be self-contained and based on Nature in equal measure.

> It is not due to chance, therefore, but in accordance with Nature's prescription, if the artist always has felt, and still feels, the perfect fifth to be more potent than the third. . . . It constitutes for the artist a unit by which to measure what he hears. The fifth is, to use another metaphor, the yardstick of the composer.[14]

The disposition of the triad in Nature also explains why the third produces a more engaging effect in the open position of the triad than in the close position. (Schenker treats the open vs. close position in *Kontrapunkt II*, p. 27.)[15] We find this disposition, to choose a few examples from many, in the Preludes in *C♯* Major and *D* Major of the first volume of the *Well-Tempered Clavier* (see examples 21 and 22).

Example 21.   Bach, *WTC I*, Prelude in C♯ Major

Example 22.   Bach, *WTC I*, Prelude in D Major

---

14. Schenker, *Harmony*, p. 26. [The word "therefore" in the first sentence refers to the sentence immediately preceding in *Harmony*, in which Schenker observes that the fifth occurs before the third in the overtone series.]

[15. Among the other observations offered there, Schenker writes that "if we may interpret Nature's purpose, it is as though she wishes at least to grant the third, as the weaker overtone, the advantage and protection of the higher position in comparison to the stronger fifth."]

A literal use occurs at the beginning of Schubert's "Meeresstille":

Example 23.   Schubert, "Meeresstille," D. 216

The triad is the simultaneity given by Nature, and the intervals that it comprises are the *consonances* given by Nature. The concepts of consonance and dissonance are more disputed today than ever before. Some go so far as to deny an essential distinction between them and recognize only a gradation, according to which the dissonances are related to the more distant overtones:

> The difference between consonance and dissonance is therefore only one of degree, not one of kind. They are no more opposites than the numbers two and ten are opposites, which follows also from their respective vibration ratios; and the terms "consonance" and "dissonance," which indicate opposition, are false. It is up to the increasing capacity of the analytical ear to become familiar with the more distant overtones and thus to extend the concept of an artistically viable euphonious sonority so as to include within it the complete natural phenomenon.[16]

That is the typically naturalistic veiwpoint of our time, which is no longer able to decide what is necessary for Art, and which therefore begins with false premises. Aside from the fact that in Art we cannot get along without conceptual opposites, the decisive factor in the classification of intervals is not at all whether or not they are "euphonious," but whether or not they are *usable* for Art. Mere habituation—and this is what Schoenberg's definition reduces to—can never establish or alter qualities. Our generation lives by the fallacy that today we find sounds attractive that once (before we grew accustomed to them) were considered abhorrent. But the whole of musical evolution contradicts this reasoning. The first attempts of polyphony were aimed at testing the various intervals with respect to their usability in voice leading; and if as a result of this testing the sixth (for example), an imperfect consonance, revealed itself to be more mobile and thus more versatile than the perfect fifth, which is static and unwieldy precisely because of its perfection—did this occur because people in the meantime grew more accustomed to the sixth as a more distant overtone? This certainly would not have lessened their familiarity with the fifths! In truth, the direction of progress was not always from the simple to the complex, but rather toward the more artistically

[16. Arnold Schoenberg, *Harmonielehre* (second edition, Vienna: Universal Edition, 1922), p. 18.]

viable and therefore the more valuable. It is just the opposite of what so many today would like to persuade us: sounds that may have been considered acceptable in the distant past were discarded because we learned to hear better. And the return, in our own time, to certain "harshnesses" of earlier idioms—what does it prove except that hearing ability has again deteriorated to the plateau of its beginnings, where it moves about helplessly in an irrational state? What a pitiful pose, to speak in this context of an "increasing capacity of the analytical ear." All that matters is *artistic* hearing ability, which means the artistic assimilation of Nature, not a purely acoustic hearing geared to the identification of as many overtones as possible. It is precisely comparable to the process of learning to see artistically, which in no way consists in turning the eye into a camera's lens. And finally, it is certainly true that two and ten are not opposites. (Incidentally, why does Schoenberg select ten, which is so familiar to us as an ordinal number, and not, for example, nineteen?) But who would deny that two to one represents a simple relationship, while [for example] nineteen to one on the contrary represents a complex, incomprehensible, and therefore unusable one?

It was mentioned earlier that the interval of the seventh is not identical to the seventh partial. That the birthplace of the seventh lies in the chord built on the fifth rather than the fundamental tone of the key may serve as a supplement to the proof cited above. If the seventh really were identical to the seventh partial, the seventh chord would have to be stable in character. In fact, the seventh chord stands for movement and calls forth movement. Moreover, the movement produced leads backward;[17] it points to the lower fifth. This by itself completely contradicts Nature, whose procreative instinct points only ahead, to the future.[18]

Recall that we found in Nature no prototype for the fourth (in relation to the fundamental), and that the second, *d*, as the ninth partial, is stronger in its relation to the third partial, whose fifth it represents, than to the lowest tone, *C*. These circumstances lead to an important discovery: *The concept of dissonance does not belong to the domain of harmony as it is presented to us by Nature,* but is derived from voice leading, which is an essential constituent of *Art*. Although a complete understanding of this fact presupposes an acquaintance with the theory of voice leading, it must be mentioned here, because otherwise an artistic comprehension of the intervals cannot be attained.

The dissonances, understood from the point of view of voice leading, are accompanied by a *compulsion* toward movement, and indeed a specific movement:

Example 24.

_____

[17. See below, section 5.]
[18. See below, chap. 3, section 7.]

The fourth (in relation to the bass):

The augmented and diminished intervals, for example:

We perceive each of these dissonant tones not as in actual relation to the lowest tone, but as a transient (passing) disturbance of the consonance that should be present above the fundamental—that is, as a purely horizontal event with melodic meaning. The law that requires resolution of the dissonance is to be understood only in the light of the dissonance's origin in the passing tone of voice leading. The passing motion, once begun, requires its continuation and completion. Otherwise it would be undirected and therefore meaningless. The dissonance always carries within it this potential of movement, even when in later periods representing more advanced states of evolution it enters freely and "unprepared." (See chapter 3, section 7.) Thus, before the concept of dissonance can be investigated, one of Schenker's basic theses, of utmost importance to his theory, must be mentioned here, apropos of the presentation of the intervals: "The dissonance is always passing, *never a chord member (Zusammenklang)*."[19]

---

19. *Jahrbuch* II, [p. 24.] The expression "interval of tension" *(Spannungsintervall)*, which has lately become common, fails to capture completely this element of motion. How appropriate the old appelation *dissonare*—literally "not to sound together *(nicht zusammenklingen)*"—was, as the opposite of *consonare*. [The last word of the quotation, *Zusammenklang*, is close to *consonare* in meaning (although different, of course, in grammatical function). My rendering of it as "chord member" requires some explanation. *Zusammenklang* would be most literally translated as *simultaneous sound*, but this would lose some meaning; indeed, it would make the assertion easily refutable, for any vertical combination is a simultaneous sound. The German term as Schenker uses it here connotes not only *sounding* together but also *belonging* together as a simultaneity in the sense of *being an independent and self-explanatory vertical structure*. This is a condition that is manifested by any consonant vertical combination, but not by a dissonant one, which in one way or another will always owe its origin to the horizontal dimension—hence, to voice leading. I know of no English expression that fully captures Schenker's present use of *Zusammenklang*. "Chord member" has obvious disadvantages, because we do for convenience speak of "seventh chord," etc. Nevertheless, there is a tradition of usage according to which not every vertical combination is called a "chord"; this is reflected even in the admittedly imprecise but quite common locution "non-chordal tone," for example. Understood in this light, Schenker's meaning may become clear: it is that *no* dissonance (including the seventh) is *ever* a "chordal" tone—that is, a tone generated by some "chordal" (and therefore vertical) principle. For further clarification, see the remark on p. 57 concerning example 84; also chap. 3, section 7.]

Section 5.   The Natural System

> No work of art is absolute, not even one created by the greatest and
> most experienced artist; however much mastery he may achieve of the
> material in which he works, he can never change its *nature*.

Goethe

Following the impulse of a tone to move to its strongest overtone, the fifth, we
arrive at a new tone, which now establishes itself as an independent agent with
its own overtones. The relationship of the new tone to the original one is given
by nature as a fifth-relationship. The fifth-relationship is the one that is in accord
with Nature. If we continue in the direction of the more remote fifths, we reach
a point at which Art, in order to maintain its comprehensibility, calls for a modification, for the imposition of a limit. The series of fifths becomes *comprehensible*
if it returns to its point of departure, and thereby achieves coherence as a whole.
At the sixth fifth in the ascending series (see example 25), there arises a contradiction between its upper fifth, *C♯*, and the point of departure, *C*.

Example 25.

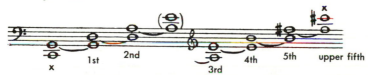

At this point, then, the limitation needed for comprehensibility had to be imposed.
In order to return to *C* in a natural way, its relationship to the tone preceding
it had to be made to appear as a natural succession. Accordingly, at the fifth
step along the path of ascending fifths a departure was made from Nature's
way in order to make Nature usable for Art. Instead of a perfect fifth, the diminished fifth was inserted here (see example 26).

Example 26.

diminished 5th

The projection of a fifth relationship in the opposite [i.e., descending] direction
is called *inversion* by Schenker.[20]

---

20. After the first step along this descending path—inversion—had been taken, the
urge to continue it was provoked. Thus the realm of the lower fifths was entered, and
alterations toward the flat side were required if perfect fifths were to be maintained.
The necessity of adjusting in relation to the upper fifths and their respective thirds then
led to equal temperament.

That the diminished fifth was introduced in order to close the circle explains its special significance as an unequivocal defining element of the system. The significance of the lower fifth [of the fundamental tone] as an avenue of return to the point of origin is likewise clarified. Thus it serves almost as an anchor, cast out by the fundamental on the opposite side in order to preclude an unchecked ascent through the upper fifths.

Two final abbreviations now had to be made in the interest of Art. First, the respective thirds of the upper fifths had to be adjusted wherever they contradicted fundamental tones already included in the system; thus $F\sharp$, for example, as the third of the second upper fifth, had to be changed to F in order to agree with the lower fifth, and so on. And last of all, when Art compressed the natural disposition of the triads into close spacing, the result was as shown in example 27.

Example 27.

scale degrees I   II   III   IV   V   VI   VII

Example 27a.

This example illustrates our *major* system, which represents a marvelous compromise between Art and Nature.

We must withal bear constantly in mind that the true organizational principle is the fifth—a literal welling-up and falling-back in fifths that is impregnated with life and movement by the primordial urge of tones. The individual fifths, as bearers of this movement, are called *scale degrees*,[21] a term that applies to them not [only] as individual tones but, at the same time, as bearers of implicit triads and as spiritual guarantors of coherence. The scale degrees that stand in a direct fifth-relationship to the fundamental, whose triads required *no modification in favor of the fundamental* [and its system of rising fifths]—scale degrees V and IV—are called *upper dominant* (or simply *dominant*) and *subdominant* [literally, *lower dominant*], respectively. The original fundamental itself is called the *tonic*. Observe how even this designation of scale degree IV [as *subdominant*] expresses the fifth relationship. Yet most important of all is its true meaning,

---

[21. In *Harmony* the original term *Stufe* was rendered as "scale-step." In the present translation I have used "scale degree," in agreement with the usage in *Free Composition*. Thus in some quotations from *Harmony*, "scale-step" is interchangeable with my "scale degree."]

[which stems from] the artificial origin of the tone *F* as the *corrective* element of the system. This must not be forgotten.

The progression I—IV—V—I unequivocally defines the point of origin and the total system, the key; it is called the *cadence.* Accordingly, composers of earlier periods like to begin their pieces with this kind of progression, a kind of exposition of the tonality, at the same time sustaining the fundamental tone so as to characterize the motion as a preliminary one, an initial stirring. (See examples 28 and 29.)

Example 28. Bach, *WTC II,* Prelude in C Major

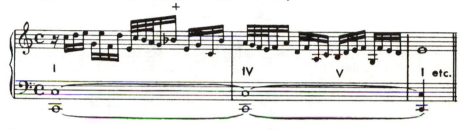

Example 29. Handel, Suite in F♯ Minor, Prelude

(Regarding the points marked + in examples 28 and 29, see section 7.)

The meaning of the cadence is this: along with motion toward the fifth (V), IV appears as a corrective, depriving V (the dominant) of its independence and pointing it back in the direction of its origin. The *F* [in the key of *C*] eliminates the possibility of hearing the *G* chord in the sense of *G* major, which would require *F♯*. This effect that the cadence produces accounts also for its use at the conclusion of a work as well as at internal rest-points that round off a particular section. When the cadence is modified in various ways, its conclusive effect is correspondingly modified, and in this light we can identify the following types of cadential articulation:

1. The perfect cadence I—IV—V—I:

Example 30. Scarlatti, Sonata in D Minor, K. 517

2. The plagal cadence I—IV—I:

Example 31.   Brahms, *Romanze,* op. 118 no. 5

which, however, leaves open the possibility of interpretation as V—I—V, and is related in this respect to the semicadence (see below).

3. The semicadence I—V (see example 32), which calls for a continuation:

Example 32.   Haydn, Sonata in B♭ Major, Hob. 41

4. The "deceptive" cadence, e.g., V—VI:

Example 33.   Mozart, Sonata in C Major, K. 330, Second Movement

which, however, takes us into the domain of voice leading.[22] We shall see how, in general, a purely melodic course of events in the upper voice corresponds to the progression of the bass tones.[23] It is upon this possibility of reconciling melodic with harmonic processes that the perfection of the major-minor system rests, as the only system which, in teleological terms, survived polyphony's natural selection process, and, in practical terms, came out of polyphony's experimental laboratory. A preliminary example, for clarification: the penultimate tone of the melodic series now established as our scale—B, which is called the leading tone to C—occurs as the third of scale degree V. Its melodic thrust toward the system's point of origin is complemented by the inclination of the fundamental, G, toward its point of origin in terms of fifth-relationships [i.e., the tonic].

It was the chord of the fifth upper fifth [see example 25], B, that was most extensively altered to satisfy the needs of the system; both its third and its fifth had to be altered. This fact accounts for the unequivocal significance of the diminished fifth in the major system, and the pull of the diminished fifth toward the tonic explains its close relation to V, for which it can often substitute, as in this example:

Example 34.   Bach, *WTC I*, Prelude in G Major

The natural movement of scale degrees is by fifths. When, in the cadence, IV stands alongside V, to which it has no direct fifth-relationship, this juxtaposition again sheds light on the artificial character of the IV. In order to avoid the juxtaposition, a favored procedure was to use II, the second fifth in the ascending series, in place of IV. (See example 35.) The triad on II, in the modified form [in which it occurs in the C-major system], also contains the tone F, if only as its third.

---

22. For further explanation see chap. 3, section 2, *c) The Fourth-Progression*, examples 111 and 112. The "imperfect cadence" cited by Schenker in *Harmony*, p. 216, in which the upper voice arrives only at the third above I, also introduces a melodic aspect into cadential considerations.

[23. The contrast that is at least implicitly drawn here between the "melodic" character of the upper voice and the "harmonic" character of the bass has to do specifically with the topic under discussion, cadences. Further on, as the concept of composing-out is developed, much emphasis will be placed upon the predominantly melodic character of the bass in tonal music.]

Example 35. Bach, *WTC I,* Prelude in D Major

Thus a compensation was provided in the progression by descending fifths through V that was thereby made available.[24] The resulting juxtaposition of I and II could be counteracted by reaching up still farther in the ladder of fifths, to VI as the third upper fifth:

Example 36. Bach, *WTC I,* Prelude in F♯ Major

With this device, however, we advance into the realm of actual voice leading, a presentation of which is deferred until later. Our purpose here is to show the power of the scale degrees—not their specific movement, but rather the force, given by nature, that leads to it. "In contrast to the theory of counterpoint," Schenker writes, "the theory of harmony presents itself to me as a purely spiritual universe, a system of ideally moving forces, born of Nature or of Art." (*Harmony,* p. xxv.)

And, once again with reference to the major-minor system, Schenker states: "No key at all could have been established, had not the way of pure Nature been abandoned, and the natural sequence of perfect fifths been adulterated with the admixture of the artificial, false, diminished fifth interval between the VII and IV steps." (*Kontrapunkt II,* p. xiii.) The artist sets out from Nature's postulate and fulfills it, but he also creates a causality for the work of art—one that is suited to it alone.

---

24. Because of its frequent occurrence, the substitution of II for IV led to the erroneous inference that II generally lacked independence and was to be understood merely as a representative of IV. This assumption caused still further confusion when it was extended, by analogy, to VI and III. This is the [essential] content of the theory of harmonic functions [as promulgated by Hugo Riemann and his followers]. That theory fails to recognize that the importance of IV and V derives from their significance as *adjacent* fifths of the tonic and from their circumscription of the tonality; and that the other scale degrees, although more distant in the ladder of fifths, nevertheless retain their independence within the system. The most persuasive argument against functional theory is offered below in section 7, *Tonicization.*

Section 6. The Artificial System and the Scale[25]

The first attempts to introduce an orientational framework into successions of tones go back to an early period. Scales were established whose initial and terminal pitches were fixed, as were the intervallic distances among the tones. These scales, or "modes," were an aid in constructing melodies; they imbued melodies, if in a primitive way, with characteristic identifying properties based on the relative positions of the whole- and half-steps. Relocation of the melodic beginning to other tones of the scale further increased the resources. When the possibility of transposition was added to this, an impressive array of such modes became available. By the end of the middle ages, the extant modes were those shown in example 37.

Example 37.

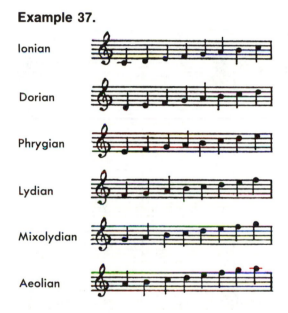

Ionian

Dorian

Phrygian

Lydian

Mixolydian

Aeolian

Thus there was always the same succession of the same seven tones; only the initial tone was variable. With the already existing attempts at polyphony, there arose effects and associated problems that could not have been anticipated. The desire for polyphony may have arisen from the natural urge of tones toward chordal fulfillment through their overtones, although at first it may have lain dormant in the subconscious and been motivated in purely practical terms by other causes—perhaps the wish to achieve greater length in melody, whose scope was limited for various reasons such as liturgical tradition and the limitations of memory. Since melody could not be extended, at least not horizontally, the

[25. *Tonreihe*. The terms *Skala* and *Tonreihe* are both used initially in this section in their most general meaning of "scalar ordering." In the third sentence the word *Tonarten* occurs, in quotation marks, with the meaning "modes." Thereafter, *Skala*, *Tonreihe*, and simply *Reihe* are all to be understood in this more specific meaning, and consequently all have been rendered as "mode."]

attempt was made to enrich it in another dimension—the vertical. As musicians learned to attend more closely to the chord and its particular requirements, the discrepancy between the implications of the mode and the will of the chord became all the more apparent. For example, the mode, in its horizontal succession, pointed clearly toward a conclusion; yet the total context tended rather to suppress a feeling of closure. A gaping chasm opened between the horizontal and the vertical. The consequence of polyphony for the birth of our system was to enable a testing of the various modes with respect to their usability. To return to the example mentioned above, the feeling for the dominant, reconciled with the leading tone of the mode as its chordal third, could be developed best of all in the Ionian mode.

Example 38.

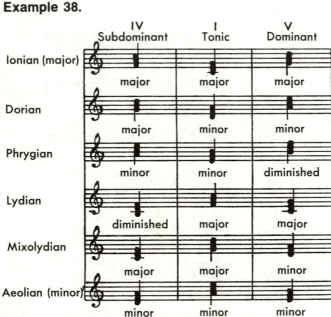

A table of the triads on I, V, and IV as they appear in the various modes (see example 38) suggests certain inferences. In the Phrygian mode we find a diminished triad on the dominant, which would tend toward a closure on degree VI; in the Lydian mode, the diminished triad appears on the subdominant; and so forth. The only mode that yields natural triads with major thirds on all three scale degrees is the Ionian—just the mode from which our major, the natural system, developed.[26]

Hand in hand with these experiments—"experiments" only from our point of view, of course; they were the compositional efforts of that period—attempts at motivic organization were also under way. It was the golden age of imitation.

---

26. It would be the task of a history of music to set forth in fuller detail what can only be hinted at here.

As the need arose to repeat the motive (here perhaps better called tone-succession) on the tone most closely related, the V, it was natural to strive for the most exact possible correspondence [between repetition and original]. A motive based on a major triad called for a repetition in kind, at least at the beginning of a work's unfolding. The same held true for a motive based on a minor triad, for example in the Aeolian or Dorian mode. Thus a second controlling factor arose, an evaluation in terms of usability in the horizontal direction. Returning to our table (example 38), we note that a congruence of minor triads on degrees I, IV, and V occurs only in the Aeolian mode; therefore the minor [scale] as a system appears to have originated in the Aeolian mode, but not in a way completely reconciled with Nature. The lack of complete agreement with Nature is indicated by the fact that the minor scale has no leading tone (from VII to I) and therefore has to borrow one from the major scale of the same letter name.

In this respect our minor system represents a compromise between Art and Nature. The leading tone is a borrowed accidental, which, despite its frequent occurrence, is not to be expressed in the key signature. How helpless and inartistic is conventional theory, which explains the absence of a key signature for *a* minor with reference to a "third relationship" to *C* major, and thus arrives at the notion of a "relative" key—as if the borrowed *g#* would not point sooner and more strongly to *A* major![27] Evidently this way of thinking is reinforced by the fact that pieces in minor often move, as they unfold, first of all to the third of the fundamental as scale degree III. But this fact has a different, more profound reason than the third relationship assumed by theorists.[28]

Another special trait of the minor system contributes to this tendency. While in major the diminished triad is located on VII, and thus the fifth ascending fifth (an advantage of the major system!), in minor it appears already on the second ascending fifth. It is just the tendency of the diminished triad toward "resolution" that makes it so easy for the minor to digress toward III. This fact was often inconvenient, especially in view of the practice noted earlier of substituting II for IV in the cadence. Thus it happened that frequently, in order to block the diminished triad's "pull," an alteration was adopted in which *b* was lowered to *bb*, producing a major chord. This is how a trait really intrinsic to the Phrygian mode was incorporated into the minor system.[29]

[27. The concepts "relative major" and "relative minor" are indeed foreign to Schenkerian thought. If, for example, an *A*-minor chord were tonicized (see section 7) within a work in *C* major, Schenker would explain it in any of several ways, depending upon the larger context: the *A* bass might be a passing tone in a descending or ascending linear progression; it might be an upper neighboring tone to V; or any of several other possibilities. He would never invoke an independent concept of "relative" keys.]

28. Compare the technique of arpeggiation [as discussed with reference to] example 47, and chap. 2, section 2.

29. Schenker names this phenomenon the "Phrygian II," instead of the customary designation "Neapolitan sixth." The fact that it is so often used as a $\frac{6}{3}$ chord is a consequence of its inclusion in the cadence, where the leap of an augmented fourth in the bass is thereby avoided.

It cannot be determined exactly when the church modes began to gravitate toward major and minor, because for a long time accidentals were applied according to tacit agreement and were not notated by the composer.[30] The mere addition of B♭ to the Lydian mode, for example, produced the effect of Ionian; adding B♭ to the Dorian mode resulted directly in the Aeolian. As the major-minor system proved capable of assimilating certain traits [of the other modes] such as the typically Phrygian one mentioned above, and characteristic features of major and minor could moreover be intermixed—what a wealth of resources, what variety was thus imparted to our system! Composers of later periods were even able to achieve archaic effects, when it suited their purposes, within the framework of the major-minor system. (See examples 39 and 40.)

Example 39.   Chopin, Mazurka op. 41 no. 1

*Phrygian

Example 40.   Brahms, *A German Requiem,* op. 45, First Movement, bars 20ff.

Only when we understand this centuries-long evolutionary process during which our system took shape,[31] when we learn that the same "modes, which had been called Ionian and Aeolian, reinterpret for artistic ends an aggregation of seven fundamental tones, organized by fifths, as scale degrees under the control of a single one among them"[32]—only then do we become fully aware of the misconcep-

---

30. Even J. S. Bach often notated with a Dorian signature pieces that were obviously composed in minor; this was simply the continuation of a tradition that had lost all meaning.

31. "Today we know that the major mode has been, so to speak, designed and ordained by Nature; and yet we needed hecatombs of artists, a universe of generations and artistic experiments, to penetrate the secrets of Nature and attain her approval. For the way by which we could approach Nature was merely our auditive sense . . . ." Schenker, *Harmony,* p. 53.

32. Schenker, *Harmonielehre,* p. 118. [Jonas has altered this quotation, without seriously affecting its meaning, to make it fit the syntax of his sentence. The translation given is a literal rendering of Jonas's quotation. The gist of the original passage is as follows: The demands of instrumental music led *composers* to reinterpret the *modes,* which had formerly been called Ionian and Aeolian, as (each) an aggregation of seven fundamental tones that assume the meaning of scale degrees under the control of one among them. The passage is translated in *Harmony,* p. 95.]

tions about art in our own time, which advocates exotic scales or manufactured "tone-rows," extolling these as necessary developments and successors to the allegedly obsolete [major-minor] system. Having seen how the old modes had to undergo necessary correction as soon as polyphony came along, how the possibility, at last made attainable, of reconciling melodic and harmonic forces became the prerequisite of the richness in our system—what can we think of an effort like the so-called "twelve-tone row," which posits an equality of value for the twelve half-steps within an octave? What a direct denial of that first, most fundamental reality of our music: the fifth!

Even if the decline of musical art, the dissolution of the tonal system, came about of necessity, it would never be valid to conclude that such necessity implies progress. Granted: because the capacity for artistic hearing has declined steadily, the natural foundation of the major system has ceased to be recognized and has no longer found creative expression in works of art. But to infer from this that the tonal quagmire of the twelve-tone row still maintains any connection to Nature—what a short circuit in thinking! As Goethe puts it, "it is as difficult to learn from models as from nature."

Section 7.   The Concept of Tonicization

We have observed that several tones within the system were forced to relinquish, for the benefit of the system as a whole, the independent life to which they would otherwise tend; they had to be integrated into the social order of the original fundamental. The adjustment required was more extensive the farther removed the tone in question was from that fundamental. The second, third, and fourth fifths in the ascending series underwent modifications of their respective thirds; the fifth fifth admitted a modification even of its fifth. Once the system was secured and stabilized within itself, however, it became possible to yield to the individual will of the tones within the confines of the system as a whole without endangering it as a totality. On the contrary: a transient and therefore merely apparent excursion into a distant region could only render service to the system, because the return simply confirms the point of departure all the more emphatically. A tone, striving for independence, seeks it in the phenomenon that Schenker calls "tonicization." The latter represents a triumph of the system, which thus proves itself capable of assimilating even the original natural [major] triads. The medium through which tonicization is implemented is *chromaticism*. A given tone, either a closer or a more distant member of the series of fifths, endeavors to appear as a principal tone.[33] It attempts this first of all in a modest way, purely melodically, without impinging on the complete harmony. This may be carried out with the aid of a simple chromatic passing tone or a [chromatic] neighboring tone; in either case, the effect produced is like that of a leading tone, as shown in example 41.

[33. *Hauptton*. The actual meaning here is *tonic*.]

Example 41. Mozart, Sonata in B♭ Major, K. 570, Last Movement

Or, on the other hand, the third of a minor triad may be raised; the resulting major triad elevates the significance of the following chord by relating to it in the manner of a dominant and by lending it briefly the value of a tonic (hence the term tonicization), as in example 42.

Example 42. Mozart, Fantasy in C Minor, K. 475, Andantino

Other possibilities are shown in the examples from Bach and Handel (examples 28 and 29) cited above in connection with the cadence. In those examples the IV gains in independence through the use of chromatically altered passing tones (*bb* and *a♯*, respectively), and the descending fifth I—IV (a case of inversion) receives motivation. The tendency of a tone to move to its fifth, mentioned earlier at the beginning of section 5, and the tendency of that fifth to manifest itself as a fundamental—these constitute the sum and substance of the tonicization process. They also provide, in fugue and sonata, the first stimulus for formal organization. The path to the dominant is illustrated in example 43.

Example 43. Haydn, Sonata in C Major, Hob. 50, Last Movement

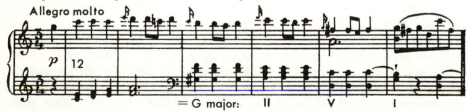

The third, *f* [of the bass *D* in bar 16] is chromatically raised to f♯; the *D* chord thus takes on a major and a dominant quality. The effect of the *A* chord is bolstered by g♯, and so there arises a progression equivalent to II—V—I in *G* major. *A* and *D*, in other words, manifest themselves rather as closer fifths of *G* than as

more distant fifths of *C*.[34] If the tonicized scale degree is itself supplied with a
major third, we [can] obtain, as in example 44, a whole series of major triads
falling by fifths (inversion), which most fittingly lend the strict [diatonic] system
an element of nature's joy in color.

Example 44.   Beethoven, Piano Concerto in G Major, op. 58

And yet, how securely the ear hears only the key of *G* major! How well it is
guided through all of the intermediate points of tension to a firm perception of
the point of departure! The measures cited are the beginning of the tutti, which
answers the piano's solo entry. One of Beethoven's sketches for the concerto
(see example 45) shows clearly how deliberately he aimed for a temporary coloration within the [diatonic] system, and how erroneous conventional theory is in
speaking of "modulation" and of other "keys."

Example 45.

In the sketch, the *B*-major chord is quite evidently a transient element which
does not interfere with the overall course of events; the orchestra enters, like
the piano before it, with a *G* chord, and the melodic line unfolds without alteration.
From this seed Beethoven's ultimate conception developed: the *B*-major chord
was relocated to the beginning of the phrase and implanted in the series of descending fifths. (We cannot here deal with the way in which this passage is founded

---

34. If we speak of *G* major here as a quasi key, we do so only for the sake of introductory
simplification; this should not be viewed as contradicting our later explanations (e.g., chap.
4, section 3) or Schenker's concept of tonality with its stipulation of unity of key over an
entire composition. See examples 44 and 45, as well as footnote 93 to chap. 3.

and integrated in voice leading and its linear progressions. See chapter 3.) It would of course be simpler to speak here of a "loosening up" of the scale *(Tonart)*, or something of the sort—a "loosening" that would necessarily lead to a "freer" style and ultimately to that of the present day. But it is much more important to focus attention on the system of constraints which, despite the chordal diversity, secures a definite course of motion. Just this system of constraints is the important thing; through it alone, all of the chords find justification.

In this connection reference must be made to a certain phenomenon that will receive fuller treatment in the next chapter. It is important because of its relevance to the question touched upon here of other theoretical explanations and, moreover, because it shows how the principle of tonicization permeates all aspects of the tonal system. In the example cited above, the tone *B*—the third of the tonic chord—presented itself as the fourth fifth in the ascending series, with its naturally-given *B*-major triad. But what is the role of III in example 46, where it again occurs as a major triad?

Example 46.   Beethoven, Sonata in C Major, op. 53, First Movement

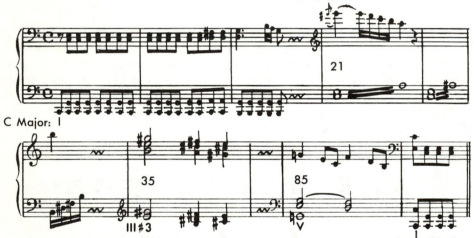

It was mentioned earlier, in our discussion of the minor system, that pieces in minor keys often move first to the third, and only afterward continue on to the fifth. An example, to choose one from many, is given below.

Example 47.   Haydn, Sonata in E Minor, Hob. 34, Last Movement

An additional reason why this plan is followed especially in minor pieces may well be that the minor third needs further confirmation; the triad in its basic form, after all, contains a major third between root and fifth. (Thus even practice itself verifies the artificial nature of minor.) The true function of the third—even in major, as in the present case—is to be understood purely as an *expansion of the path from the tonic to its fifth.* The third is assimilated in this way and occurs in the arpeggiation of the triad. Under no circumstances can we speak of an independent third relationship, one that would negate the primal component of the system, the fifth. This fact is unaltered by the tonicization process, as shown in the example from Beethoven's op. 53 (example 46), where the third is supplied with a chromatic tone and is even expanded to provide the tonal region for the second theme.

To state precisely the difference between examples 44 and 46: in the former case the third is embedded in a progression of descending fifths (inversion); in the latter it is a way-station and divider of a fifth. Classical music knows both cases, and if the second of them—especially in major keys—came to be highly favored by later composers (Schubert, for example), there is no cause to see in this a preparation for modern harmony. The point is to hear through to the underlying connections rather than stopping at the individual sonority.[35]

The principle of tonicization is, moreover, particularly well suited to expose the error of the theory of functional harmony,[36] which grants independence only to degrees I, IV, and V. If this were the case, the descending succession of tonicized fifths VI—II—V—I in example 44 would be impossible and incomprehensible. And as soon as the more distant fifths retrieve their respective chromatically altered tones, as happens in tonicization, the alleged relationship of I and VI (as well as II and IV, and also V and III) disintegrates. If the thirds of the more distant fifths had to be "tempered" for the benefit of the system, this did not negate the *organization* according to fifths; and, as our examples show, even

---

35. [Ernst] Kurth fails to do this in his *Romantische Harmonik [und ihre Krise in Wagners Tristan* (Bern, 1920)]. Kurth too severely limits his premises to individual phenomena, and thus is able to reach the conclusion that the system had to undergo a loosening and finally a complete dissolution as a "logical consequence."

[36. Cf. chap. 1, footnote 24.]

the [natural] thirds themselves can always be used when appropriate. (See *Kontra-punkt I*, p. 36ff.)

It has often been necessary in this chapter to refer to later topics, and finally, in connection with the concept of arpeggiation, even to take things out of order. This merely confirms the oft-stated precept that the principles of harmony are purely spiritual—that the scale degree is a spiritual driving force, a bequest from Nature to Art; a force that manifests itself and attains realization in the work of art through those means that are proper to Art. This explains why Schenker, in his *Harmony*, was able to develop his concepts only with reference to examples taken from living works, and why he excluded all exercises of the conventional variety.

Chapter 2

The Artistic Formation of the Chord

Section 1. Unfolding of the Chord in Time

In the concluding part of the preceding chapter reference had to be made to a phenomenon that now requires a more detailed discussion. As soon as the topic of rhythm arose, the unfolding of music in time was mentioned; and this leads to a new problem: how was the triad, which in the overtone series represents a vertical—and thus simultaneous—phenomenon, to be fructified over a span of time without either being simply repeated or being supplanted by another triad? The [tonal] system shows us only the selection of triads and their natural and logical succession. The single triad, however, is without individual life and without form. A spatial entity, it needs to be vitalized in time. This is provided by *composing-out (Auskomponierung)*. In its conversion from a vertical arrangement into a horizontal one, the triad is transformed from a spatial into a temporal entity. The first technique of composing-out is arpeggiation (see example 48).

Example 48.

Composing-out represents the decisive breakthrough in musical evolution. It alone permitted the establishment of a relationship and a connection between temporally disparate points. Arpeggiation generates *tonal space;* it can determine the beginning- and end-point of a musical occurrence. Schenker, in his "Explanations," writes the following:

The chord of nature is the *triad:*

Example 49.

Because art is a human product, the limited compass of the human voice alone requires that consideration be given only to the abbreviated form of the natural chord:

Example 50.

which, when its tones are presented in succession, establishes *tonal space.*[1]

The nature-given interval, with its capacity to generate tonal space, represents a virtual "a priori" of the ear. Only under the assumption that the work of art must necessarily fill in this natural interval can it offer the possibility of tension, expectation, fear of non-fulfillment, and ultimate fulfillment. Every artistic formation and effect depends on the obligation created by tonal space.

By means of composing-out, then, a vertical entity can manifest itself and be realized also as a succession. The significance of this concept is presented in Schenker's *Harmony*, where, in the chapter Scale-Steps and Contents,[2] we read:

In practical art the main problem, in general, is how to realize the concept of harmony (of a triad or seventh chord) in a live content. In Chopin's Prelude op. 28 no. 6, thus, it is the motive:

Example 51.   Chopin, Prelude in B Minor, op. 28 no. 6

that gives life to the abstract concept of the triad, *B, D, F♯*; whereas

Example 51a.

[1. Schenker, *Jahrbuch I*, p. 203.]
[2. See chapter 1, footnote 21.]

would have the effect of an assertion merely sketched for the time being.[3]

The art of composing-out chords forms the sum and substance of the masterworks. Its abandonment, the return to writing chords as empty shells, signifies the abandonment of the musical essence.[4] Only composing-out is able to do justice in an *organic* fashion to music as temporal art. It establishes coherence at the local level—in the motive—, in the thematic group, and finally in the large form. The first path to composing-out is arpeggiation of the chord. Example 52 illustrates arpeggiation as a vehicle of the motive.

Example 52.   Mozart, Sonata in A Minor, K. 310

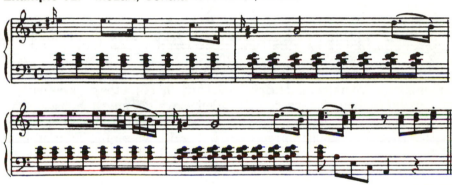

A sketch by Beethoven of the first theme of the Eighth Symphony together with the theme itself shows how a finely honed, almost chiselled melodic line emerges from a simple arpeggiation, initially only rhythmically shaped:

Example 53.

a)

b)

On the other hand, an arpeggiation can also mark off the tonal space for the continuation of the composition:

3. Schenker, *Harmony*, [pp. 211–212].
4. See footnote 110 to chap. 3.

Example 54. Beethoven, Sonata in B♭ Major, op. 106

The arpeggiation from the third (bar 1) to the fifth (bar 3) is the decisive component of the musical content. The space that it delineates becomes the space in which the subsequent motivic elaboration in bars 5–10 unfolds (compare example 87). This space is next expanded to reach bb^4 in bar 17, where the B♭ triad finds its initial fulfillment. Each triadic tone is embellished with its auxiliary note (see chapter 3, section 3). The upward arpeggiation is answered by the downward arpeggiation in bars 27ff. (See example 55.[5])

Example 55.

Mozart outlines the space of a *C*-major triad in his Sonata in *C* Major, K. 309:

---

5. In Schenker's diaries, which came into my possession in 1963, there is the following entry of August 26, 1925: "As I was out walking I hit upon some excellent improvements in understanding the magnificent synthesis of Op. 106, first movement: at the very beginning the arpeggiation d^3–f^3–bb^3 and then back, bb^3–f^3–d^3; also extremely important ideas about the fugue." (Unfortunately Schenker never returned to his study of the Sonata op. 106.) [However, an unpublished, detailed analysis of the fugue, virtually completed by Schenker, is contained in the Oster Collection at the New York Public Library, Division of the Performing Arts.]

Example 56. Mozart, Sonata in C Major, K. 309

How marvelous the arpeggiation in the right hand's grace-note figure, which finds its continuation as though in a great arc! A proof, again, that in the master-work even an ornament is not a mere appendage but participates in the total synthesis. (Compare examples 5, 6, and 57.) Observe too the variety in composing-out of the individual small partial arpeggiations indicated in example 56b. (Compare also example 73.) Only composing-out engenders hearing that binds tones together. It causes retention in consciousness of a melodic point of departure beyond the limits of its actual sonic duration, as though it were actually sustained. Because of this, it is possible to hook on once again to the point of departure and to ensure continuity:

Example 57. Haydn, Variations in F Minor

Observe the mission of the appoggiatura c^3 in bar 4, which touches again on the c^3 of the beginning.[6] It is in terms of the spirit of tonal space and its compositional unfolding that we must understand that passage in the alleged Mozart letter which portrays his creative process so vividly:

> And the thing becomes really almost finished in my mind, even if it is long, so that thenceforth I can see it at a glance, as if I were looking at a beautiful picture or a comely person; and I can hear it in my imagination, *not in temporal succession*, as will always be necessary in performance, but *as if all at once*.[7]

The preceding remarks about the implicit sustaining of an individual tone applies even more to the spiritual driving force of the scale degree. The fundamental tone of the scale degree manifests itself even without having to be continuously physically present. And composed-out chords need not always be scale-degree chords—that is, chords that partake of the tonality and therefore represent the highest category.[8] The tonal space as goal and plan of construction becomes the progenitor of musical form. Consider in this connection examples 7–9. How clearly

---

6. Compare also the arpeggiation, represented in *Jahrbuch II* [Anhang III, Fig. 2], of Haydn's Sonata in *G* Minor [Hob. 44]. And see below, chap. 3, section 2, *g*) ''Conjunction and Alignment of Linear Progressions.''

7. The authenticity of this letter has been widely disputed, and probably with justification. This alters nothing of the rare beauty of its content. Goethe once said to Eckerman that things must be judged not by whether or not they are true, but whether or not they have *meaning*. Let this apply to our letter!

8. This is the foundation of Schenker's later theory of strata. (See p. 138.)

Mozart's intended filling-out of the tonal space *f–a* in the *d*-minor triad reveals itself![9]

Section 2.   The Bass as Vehicle of the Arpeggiation

One might ask what became of polyphony as horizontalization developed—whether it would perhaps necessarily have had to be sacrificed. For all that this question is justified, its answer must be deferred until the next chapter, which is devoted to voice leading. Here our aim is first of all to gain familiarity with the phenomenon of arpeggiation in and for itself, independent of its consequences for the total musical fabric. Still, we can approach the problem more closely if we distinguish whether the arpeggiation is carried out by the lowest voice in the setting or by some other voice. We learned earlier that the tone aspires to appear as a fundamental, and even to be accompanied by its own overtones. (This fact alone decides in favor of polyphony.) It is clear that this aspiration is most prominent in the case of the lowest voice, and it is this circumstance that accounts for the superior significance of the bass in polyphonic settings.[10]

---

9. Other instances of the concept of motivic composing-out are the two examples cited by Schenker in *Harmony* with reference to the topic of inversion:

Example 58. Haydn, Sonata in A♭ Major, Hob. 46

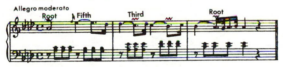

Example 59. Mozart, Sonata in F Major, K. 332

The latter example shows how a diversity of composing-out can be achieved even by the simplest intervallic inversion; bars 3 and 4 really stand for:

Example 60.

10. "I cannot recommend strongly enough the study of the bass motions in the works of J. S. Bach. One should begin with the *Generalbass-Büchlein* and attempt to ascertain the linear progressions implied in these seemingly simple basses. . . ." Schenker, *Free Composition*, p. 75.

Consider the following example:

Example 61.   Chopin, Prelude in F Major, op. 28 no. 23

The triad could be compared to an organism. Just as a body, apparently at rest, becomes animated and takes on all manner of shapes and configurations as soon as it moves by activating muscle and joint, so the triad, originally idle and self-contained, becomes buoyant and agile when it begins to move muscle and joint, to oscillate and vibrate, shaping and connecting time and space, until it comes to rest once more.[11]

We can trace this course of events in the left-hand part of example 61. In bar 1, the triad at rest (note the position of the chord, with the third on top); in

---

11. Compare examples 51 and 51a.

bar 2, motion through the fifth to the third; in bar 3 the same motion accelerated; then in bar 5 the fifth finally imposes its own triad—a *C* triad—, repeating within its framework the same sequence of events, and ultimately returning again to *F*, now an octave higher. In summary, then:

Example 62.

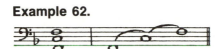

Above and beyond all of the small (motivic) arpeggiations, the large one within the *F* triad. The fifth actually becomes the "joint" of the harmony. It divides the path to the octave and facilitates departure from and return to the fundamental. Schenker terms the arpeggiation I—V—I the *upper-fifth divider.*[12] The divider is an important determining factor for the disposition of content. Because it describes a primal movement, it is directly comprehensible to the ear, whether it occurs on a small scale as in example 63

Example 63.   Schubert, Waltz op. 9 no. 17

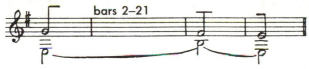

or in bar 4 of example 6, or on a larger and more expansive one, as in example 4, bars 1–23–24:

Example 64.

bars 2–21

The divider produces inner connection and makes possible the retention in memory of the point of departure.[13] As we have seen, this is independent of length, and it is also independent of whether or not the harmony of the fifth itself is built up into a larger complex. (See the discussion below of sonata form [especially p. 142f.]) This is merely an instance of the general principle that duration in music plays no role in determining the significance of an event so long as the

[12. *Oberquintteiler.* This word was erroneously omitted from the second German edition. The middle term, V, is the divider.]

[13. The divider has this property by virtue of its position as the first overtone of the fundamental; the motion from the tonic to its fifth delineates the tonic itself, and accordingly facilitates its retention in memory as a latent presence.]

foundational pillars are so placed as to be capable of supporting the superstructure. The concept of the divider can also provide insight into the hierararchic order of triads—their "stratification":

Example 65.

The fifth, only temporarily stabilized, returns once again to the origin, provides it with clarification, and relates to it as a *secondary* element. This formation, projected over an entire composition, further illuminates the essential nature of tonality.

In the next chapter the divider-concept will gain added depth; but first, it is appropriate here to mention certain derivative types of bass arpeggiation.

First of all, the motion to the fifth can be expanded, as already mentioned in connection with the minor mode, to include the third in the arpeggiation. The arpeggiation then delineates a complete triad. Examples of this type of bass arpeggiation in minor can be found easily. To the one already cited (example 47) may be added several that take place in a larger format. Consider, for example, the disposition of tonal areas in the *c*-minor Fugue of the first book of the *Well-Tempered Clavier:*

Bar:	1	11	17	22
	c	*E♭*	*g*	*c*
	I	III	V	I

(Among many other examples, compare also from Book II of the *Well-Tempered Clavier* the Fugue in *F♯* Minor, the Preludes in *C* Minor and *F* Minor, etc.) Or the plan in Beethoven's Piano Sonata in *F* Minor, op. 57, first movement:

Bar:	1	35	123	151
	f	*A♭*	*c*	*f*
	I	III	V	I

(In addition, [the first movements of] Beethoven's Symphony no. 5, Mozart's Quintet in *G* minor, K. 516, etc.) In these examples we see how the arpeggiation extends over the course of the entire composition and exerts an influence on its formal organization (the tonality concept!).

In major-key pieces, the motion to the fifth less frequently touches on the third. The appeal of such a procedure often lies in the fact that the triad on the third scale degree in major is a minor chord, and thus affords a welcome change of color:

Example 66. Chopin, Impromptu in F# Major, op. 36

The *a#*-minor triad in this example is, moreover, tonicized. Compare, among other examples, Brahms's Waltz op. 39, no. 15; Intermezzo in *Ab*, op. 76, no. 3; Intermezzo in *E*, op. 116, no. 4; also, in the *Variations on a Theme by Handel*, op. 24, variations 11, 14, and 19.

On the other hand, the minor triad on degree III in major can be transformed to major and be shaped in a still more colorful way. This is the case in example 46 above from Beethoven's Sonata op. 53. Schubert's fondness for this "third-route" in major keys need hardly be mentioned.

The path to the third can itself be lengthened and expanded. It is obvious that an expansion is required when the triad on the third scale degree is to be tonicized, as in example 46. But there is also another possible means of expansion—one that uses interval inversion. Instead of arriving directly at the third, the path can lead [downward] through the spatially larger sixth to reach the third in the lower octave. This method of expansion is to be understood in the same way even if, as in example 67, the low *Eb* is set not with an *Eb* chord but with a *c*-minor chord in $\frac{6}{3}$ position.

Example 67. Mozart, String Quartet in C Major, K. 465, Introduction

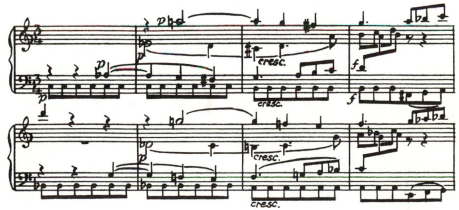

The stepwise approach to this Eb^6 [14] will be explained in more detail later. (See chapter 3, section 2d, "sixth-progression," example 115.)

A marvelous expansion within a *C* triad is found in Schubert's song *"Meeresstille."* The third of the triad, realized as an *e*-minor chord, arrives only [in bar 25] at the words *"In der ungeheuren Weite"*;[15] it leads through the fifth, in the penultimate bar, back to the fundamental in the last bar. Varieties of coloration can accompany the third-arpeggiation through the use of mixture; the effect will vary according to whether the chord quality used (major or minor) corresponds to or contrasts with the one that would be expected in a given case. Thus Brahms, at *"denn es wird die Posaune schallen"* in the *German Requiem*, passes from a *c*-minor harmony through nothing less than *e*-minor. In Schubert's song *"Auf dem Flusse"* the following variants are found:

Example 68.

Compare also Chopin's Prelude in *E* major, op. 28, no. 9, with its arpeggiation through the Ab ($G\sharp$) sound, and also through the *G* sound in the penultimate bar; further, Beethoven, Piano Sonata in *G*, op. 31, no. 1, first movement.

Apropos of the construction of the tonal system it was shown how the path to the fifth below the tonic was discovered through artificial imitation (the process of inversion). By the same token, arpeggiation through the upper fifth as divider can now be imitated by arpeggiation through a *lower-fifth divider*. While in the case of *c–g–c* our ear is clearly oriented with respect to the point of origin, *c–f–c* (as was observed in relation to the plagal cadence) leaves open the possibility that the effect is V—I—V in *F* major. In this respect, the dividing lower fifth requires further clarification by the context, and therefore it cannot always suffice to regulate the disposition of content for a whole composition. Accordingly, it

---

[14. A $\frac{6}{3}$ chord above Eb bass, not to be confused with a "first inversion" of an Eb triad.]

[15. This reading, which appeared also in the first German edition, is at variance with a later one by Jonas published in his appendix to Schenker's *Harmony*, p. 347. The later reading, which I regard as better, interprets the bass of the F-major chord at the words *"glatte Fläche rings umher"* as an upper neighbor between the *E*'s of bar 8 and bar 25.]

represents arpeggiation of a secondary category. (Compare chapter 3, section 3a, example 137.)

The arpeggiation to the lower fifth, too, can be divided at the third (see example 69).

Example 69. Schubert, Waltz op. 127 no. 1

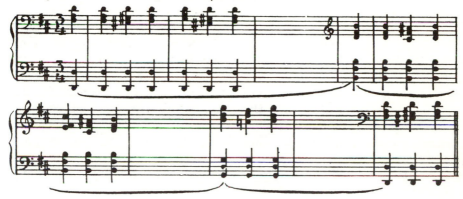

This arpeggiation has the advantage of keeping the dominant in reserve. Beethoven often used it on a large scale in his later works; as a result, he was able to withhold the arrival of the dominant, with a much more impressive effect, until the end of the development just before the beginning of the recapitulation. In op. 106, the plan is as follows:

Example 70.

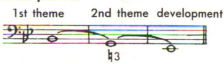

A similar procedure is used in the Piano Trio in B♭, op. 97, and the Sonata in C Minor, op. 111. Beethoven also follows this plan in the Ninth Symphony, first movement; in that case, because the movement begins with V an immediate progression back to the dominant would not have been possible. Example 71 illustrates a simple lower-fifth divider.

Example 71. Mozart, Symphony in E♭ Major, K. 543, Second Movement

In the chapter Various Kinds of Step Progression in *Harmony* [pp. 232–240],
Schenker made reference to this usage. It is true that in that exposition he still
included progressions by seconds, which belong to the domain of voice leading;
but even there he characterized them as *artificial,* in contrast to the natural
progressions based on fifths. He does characterize the motion by thirds as natural,
but less so [than that by fifths], because it is based on the fifth partial. I maintain,
however, that any natural quality of the motion by thirds is to be traced first
of all to the triadic arpeggiation. Incidentally, Schenker himself later writes, "The
psychological effect of the progression by thirds is quite often that it makes progression by fifths (upward or downward) appear as though it were divided into
two phases."[16] Thus even in *Harmony* Schenker refers to the tonal plan of Beethoven's Sonata op. 106 mentioned above in connection with example 70, and he
cites as a parallel case the Piano Quintet op. 34 by Brahms, where the "sum
total of the keys" *(sic!)* from the first theme through the second theme to the
development yields *F—Db—Bb.*[17] How deeply Schenker had penetrated into the
essence of the horizontal unfolding of triads—his most original discovery—already
in *Harmony* is revealed at a glance by an example presented in connection with
the deceptive cadence:

Example 72.   Bach, *WTC I,* Prelude in C♯ Minor

He adds beneath the *A♯* in the bass of bar 35, which is designated as raised
VI, the parenthesized remark "II^x3 already developing."[18] Thus he clearly indicates
the composing-out (development) *A♯—F✕—D♯* of the bass in bars 2–4!

The above examples have perhaps established sufficiently how arpeggiation,
as the transformation of vertical sounds into temporal events, represents a possible
source of artistic coherence in music. One additional topic should be mentioned
briefly. It points ahead to the next chapter, which deals with voice leading; thus
the following paragraphs may serve as a transition.

[16. Schenker, *Harmony,* p. 235.]
[17. Schenker, *Harmony,* pp. 248–249.]
[18. Schenker, *Harmony,* p. 222.]

Section 3. The Filling-In of the Arpeggiation

Consider once again the first five bars of the *C*-Major Sonata by Mozart in example 56a. The tones of the arpeggiation are themselves motivically expanded, again with small downward arpeggiations, which however are subjected to modifications (example 56b). Whereas the first two motivic arpeggiations each occupy a single bar each, the third is extended to form a three-bar group. This results from the fact that the second tone of the arpeggiation is not reached directly, but instead the third *g—e* is filled in with the intermediate tone *f.* Bar 2 already shows a first attempt at such a filling-in; observe the parallelism of bar 2 and bars 3–5:

Example 73.

The arpeggiation, which even as a temporal succession remains a harmonic event, is enriched by a *melodic* event. Only now, with the aid of the *passing tone,* does it become possible to shape melodic lines. Nevertheless, the chordal arpeggiation, the nature-given interval, will always remain the necessary prerequisite for orientation of the ear. The passing tone represents a filling-in of the arpeggiated interval and serves only to effect a relationship between the tones of the arpeggiation. The *fundamental line (Urlinie)*[19] gauges the tonal spaces of the triad and, by so doing, provides its first true expression.

Example 74.

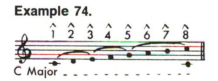

The fundamental line is the *first passing-tone motion,* and, as such, the first *melodic line* and also *diatony.*[20]

"There are no tonal spaces other than $\hat{1}$—$\hat{3}$, $\hat{3}$—$\hat{5}$, $\hat{5}$—$\hat{8}$; there is no other source of passing tones or of melody than these tonal spaces."[21]

---

19. See chap. 4.
[20. See Schenker, *Free Composition*, pp. 4 and 11.]
21. Schenker, *Jahrbuch II*, p. 195.

Chapter 3

Voice Leading and the Unfolding of the Triad

Section 1.   The Passing Tone in Strict Counterpoint and in Free Composition

Every artistically ordered succession of events in music has at its foundation a vertical concept *(Idee)*. This concept, which is kept permanently present and active by the overtone series, permeates all of our art music, regardless of whether the vertical aspect is presented as such or only indirectly, as succession. There is no art music that is merely monophonic in content. We can construe an arpeggiation in the following way:

Example 75.

The tones describe strata within the triad—the individual tonal spaces, to be precise—, and the arpeggiation leaps through these various strata, which continue to sound simultaneously in an ideal sense. The strata can, however, also be simultaneously *realized* to the extent that each stratum executes its own arpeggiation and unfolds its own tonal space:

Example 76.

The structure of this simultaneous unfolding is the subject matter of the laws of *counterpoint*. "Strict counterpoint" teaches us which *intervals* the moving voices may form and what type of motion may be used in approaching them. Because counterpoint begins with an elementary reality of nature—the overtone series—it has lasting validity. Beethoven called it an "eternal religion."

The contemporary age has succeeded in discrediting [the theory of] counterpoint, either declaring it to be obsolete or, by remodelling it for contemporary ends, depriving it of its true sense. In response, it must be said that the laws of counterpoint were discovered at a time when triadic composing-out in our sense was unknown, when each simultaneity of tones was really nothing more than a simultaneity without relationship in the horizontal plane. The ear, uninfluenced by what preceded or followed, could devote its full sensitivity and attention to the effect of the individual chord and its most felicitous connection by the individual chord-forming voices. But this is exactly the kind of school for the ear that our counterpoint-study[1] represents! The law of consonance[2] and the essential distinction between consonance and dissonance—only within the framework of this study, uninfluenced by the additional factors that enter in free composition, can they be truly grasped. The consonance as foundation of music is presented by the first species of contrapuntal theory.[3] The cantus firmus—the given voice—serves as a small exercise-platform; each of its tones has its own particular weight:[4]

Example 77. Schenker, *Kontrapunkt I*, p. 236

Second species already represents an important advance: the cantus-firmus tone is *sustained* while the other voice moves ahead. Dissonance enters for the first time, specifically as a *passing tone*. The consonant interval on the strong beat has the power to reach beyond itself and to establish larger connections. The unit of construction of the counterpoint has been expanded; it has been subjected

---

[1. In the tradition of Fux's *Gradus ad parnassum*, as described in this chapter.]

[2. *Das Gesetz der Konsonanz.* In the present context this means in general the absolute priority for vertical relation of consonance over dissonance and the attendant system of constraints on dissonance that ensues from it.]

3. The following discussion may show how unsurpassable the method of counterpoint pedagogy introduced by Fux in his *Gradus*, with its five "species," is as a signpost for art; for its organization is based on nothing other than the gradual introduction of the dissonance. When will we finally recognize that what served Haydn and Beethoven can also satisfy our needs?

[4. And, significantly, the tones of the cantus firmus are all of *equal* weight, in contrast to the situation in a melodic line of free composition, where repetition, rhythmic differentiation, and harmonic considerations assign varying degrees of weight to the individual tones. In example 77 the lower voice is the cantus firmus (originally written by Fux), the upper voice an added counterpoint (by Schenker); together they form an exercise in first-species counterpoint.]

to *prolongation.* And accordingly the law of consonance has been subjected to prolongation: it now applies not at the level of tone to tone but at the level of unit to unit, which in strict counterpoint is represented by the cantus-firmus tone:

Example 78.

As the tone receives its own elaboration, which came to pass naturally in the course of musical evolution, the law of consonance gains extended application—extended, that is, in the sense of prolongation. A small example:

Example 79.   Bach, Menuett, BWV 843

Whether we trace this prolonged structure back to the simplest two-voice basic form (a) or to a three-voice (b) or even a four-voice model (c), which latter reveals most clearly the result of the composing-out, one thing remains the same: the *C* in the bass is a passing tone, whether consonant (a) or dissonant (b, c).

It is one of the most valuable services of Schenkerian theory to have revealed for the first time the unity of composing-out and the prolonged application and validity of the laws of voice leading. What a unique gift, and what prodigious experience, were required to be able to hear through all of the elaborations of composing-out!—and those elaborations, indeed, are part and parcel of the master-works. To learn and to teach others how to hear synthetically, to be able to follow that miraculous flight of the masters, is the main goal of Schenker's work. For the masterwork is no mere concatenation of individual sound-events, but a magnificent *unfolding* of a single sound.

It is the fundamental error of conventional theory to overlook completely the law of prolongation. When theorists tried to apply the procedural "rules" of the most basic category—the "first species," so to speak—directly to the prolonged situation of the work of art, they found no agreement [between the rules and the work]. Unable to hear through to the underlying prototype, they found it easy to dismiss the study of counterpoint as an obsolete superfluity which, although perhaps still good enough to fill up lesson periods in academies and conservatories (possibly for fugal writing!) had virtually no significance for practice. The reason? Simply that theory crawled along the ground, while the masters, by virtue of laws, had learned to fly! This can easily be illustrated with a small example. Ernst Kurth, in his *Grundlagen des linearen Kontrapunkts* (what a contradiction in the very title!) writes the following about the excerpt cited in example 79 above: "According to harmonic [!] propriety, a tone such as the *d* marked + [indicating the last eighth-note of bar 28] would have to be treated as a passing tone or a neighboring tone, especially when the bass is so strictly confined to harmony tones [?!]. . . . The fact that the tone *d* leaps freely from the harmonic [!!] tone *c*. . . ."[5] Kurth thus fails to hear that the upper voice [of the first complete bar] presents a composing-out of the fifth from *a* to *d*, within which the penultimate eighth-note *e* represents a passing tone that for purely rhythmic reasons coincides with the passing *c* of the bass to yield, coincidentally, a consonant interval. The counterpoint could also read as follows:

Example 80.

Kurth thinks in terms of the rule "note against note," therefore hears *c* and *e* incorrectly as really belonging together, and then remarks that Bach, with his "ingenuity," pays no attention to such silly rules! Kurth himself stops just at the "first species," and can therefore characterize the teaching method of [species] counterpoint so glibly as "methodological confusion" and "empty schematicism." Hasn't Kurth himself fallen victim to "schematicism?" And in such a simple case, in which he neglected only one minor detail—the necessity to eliminate [for purposes of understanding] the simple composing-out and to understand the prolongation [as such].

Second species counterpoint also provides a first introduction to the concept of composing-out. The passing tone establishes a connection between the two tones of the interval [within which it moves]; it represents a melodic bridge, and generates coherence. It is the horizontal event in music:

Example 81.

As such it sets up relationship and connection between two tones of the horizontal succession without, however, entering into a separate vertical relationship to the sustained tone.

Let us for the moment remain with the concept of prolongation. If we view example 81 as the most elemental form of passing motion, the so-called "combined species" category of three-voice counterpoint, in which two voices in half notes stand against the whole note[s] of the cantus firmus, provides an extension which—properly understood—affords a deep insight into the nature of free composition.

[5. Ernst Kurth, *Grundlagen des linearen Kontrapunkts. Bachs melodische Polyphonie* (Bern: Krompholz & Co., 1917), p. 513. The bracketed interpolations are by the author.]

The procedural rule here stipulates that if the two added counterpoints move in passing tones dissonant with the cantus firmus, these two voices shall be *consonant* with each other:

Example 82.

The added voices together, then, form an independent two-voice counterpoint. If we imagine the cantus-firmus tone to be replaced by the fundamental of a composed-out triad, we obtain a picture characteristic of free composition.[6]

Example 83.

In example 83, we understand the composing-out of the *B♭* triad whether the low *B♭* is actually presented or only ideally posited. The second third, *C–E♭*, even though consonant in itself, is nevertheless to be conceived as a dissonant passing event (in relation to the ideally posited *B♭*). The consistency, from its origin, of Schenker's theory of prolongation becomes clear when we consider how its author paved the way for it as early as *Harmony*. There, we read:

> Free composition, then, appears as an extension *(Verlängerung)* [!] of strict composition: an extension with regard to both the quantity of tone material and the principle of its motion. All these extensions derive from the concept of the scale step. Under its aegis, counterpoint and free composition are wedded.[7]

---

6. "We are brought closest to free composition by the observation that the passing tones, when several of them move simultaneously, enter into a kind of obligato two-voice counterpoint of their own; that is, for purposes of their own clarification, they adopt consonance as the principle of their relation." Schenker, *Kontrapunkt II*, p. xv.

7. Schenker, *Harmony*, p. 159 [Translation modified. The interpolation in square brackets is by the author.] Even earlier, in an essay on Bruckner published in 1896, Schenker wrote as follows:

> The great masters grasped the laws of counterpoint from their psychological foundations up and, in a manner consistent with those foundations, discovered ever new paths in creative work—paths upon which freedom of creativity and the rediscovered sense of the contrapuntal rules were united. In Bruckner's case, it seems to me, freedom of creativity and the rules of counterpoint are two different things.

[Originally published in *Die Zeit*. Reprinted in *Der Dreiklang* 7 (October, 1937), pp. 166–172, the quotation above on p. 168.] And in *Harmony*, p. 177, Schenker tells of his studies with Bruckner, who used to say (in Austrian dialect), "Look, gentlemen, this is the rule. Of course, I don't compose that way."

This is then amplified in the following illustration:[8]

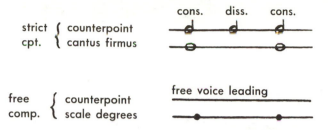

If for "scale degrees" we substitute fundamentals of composed-out chords (which are not necessarily the same), and if in addition we invoke the picture derived from the three-voice setting above [examples 82 and 83], as follows:

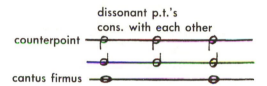

we gain a complete insight into the relation between strict counterpoint and free composition.

For clarification, two examples may be cited from *Harmony:*

Example 84. Bach, Prelude in E Minor for Organ, BWV 548

Schenker writes:

> The construct *F♯ A, B, D♯* in measure 2 could by itself stand for the second inversion of a seventh chord on *B* and, as such, for an independent fifth scale degree of *E* minor. But the *E* that is maintained on each second and fourth eighth-note of the bass and on each third quarter-note of the upper counterpoint suppresses such an interpretation. Here it is correct to hear only one scale degree, specifically the first one *(E–G–B)*, whose root, *E*, and fifth, *b*, are sustained, while *F♯* and *A* pass through [!] in the second bar, moving in parallel thirds (or tenths), as shown in the following illustration:[9]

[8. Schenker, *Harmonielehre*, p. 204; the illustration was not included in *Harmony*.]

[9. Schenker, *Harmony*, p. 142 (translation modified). The bracketed interpolation is by the author.]

Example 85.

and next:

Example 86.   Bach, Partita for Violin in D Minor, BWV 1004, Chaconne

It is especially the *D* in measure 217 of this example, which, by following immediately upon the sixth-chord, *E, G, C♯*, makes it clear at once that these three notes are passing notes and do not announce at this point any VII (or V) step and that we must hear the whole deployment of harmonies in measures 1–3 as constituting only one scale-step, viz., the composed-out [!!] I in *D* minor.[10]

In any event, in both of these examples it is the sustained tones that are reminiscent of cantus-firmus tones, when we leave the motivic elaboration out of consideration. The example cited above [in examples 17 and 18] from Mozart's *A*-Major Sonata, K. 331, goes still further; there, the fundamental, *A*, of the first measure is to be thought of as remaining in effect beneath the passing third *B–D* of the second bar. The passing event in the following example achieves still greater independence:

Example 87.   Beethoven, Sonata in B♭ Major, op. 106

Here the third *c–e♭*,[11] a passing dissonance with respect to the *B♭* triad, is enhanced with its own motivically composed-out *C* triad. (See examples 54 and 83.)

Counterpoint teaches us to hear, behind the *phenomenal* world of the work of art (which Schenker calls the foreground), the *causal* world (the background).

[10. Schenker, *Harmony*, p. 143. The bracketed interpolation is by the author.]

[11. This third is expressed as the tenth *e♭*[2] above *c*[1] at the beginning of bar 6. The carats in the example mark the main melodic tones.]

It teaches us how, instead of laboriously feeling our way chord by chord, to hear coherence and longer-span connection in tonal space. A further example:

Example 88. Beethoven, Sonata in D Minor, op. 31 no. 2, Last Movement

This excerpt is based on the following voice leading:

Example 88a.

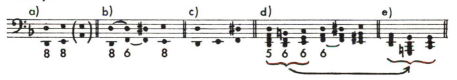

As the *d*-minor triad is led (at the end of the example) to the *E*-major, which serves as dominant of the following *A* harmony, the bass, in order to avoid consecutive octaves,[12] moves to *F*, while *d* of the upper voice progresses chromatically to *d♯*. The space of a third, *D—F*, in the bass is then filled with the passing tone *e* (see c in example 88a). The voice leading, which [at the next stage of development] is to be construed as a progression in sixths (see d), provides a basis for a further enhancement of the passing tone: instead of the $\frac{6}{3}$ chord *e–*

---

12. See chap. 3, section 7.

g–c, *C* appears in the bass by inversion, and this *C* is itself composed-out in the sense of a *C* triad.[13]

The dissonant passing tone has become a composed-out triad that has even been tonicized. Nonetheless, the *necessity* of its appearance, its logical place in context, is to be attributed *only* to the *passing tone*. This example is certainly more difficult to hear, but it also gives us an extremely important illumination of the dissonant-passing-tone concept: the dissonance itself is sterile. As a passing tone it is, to be sure, a vehicle of composing-out; but to be itself composed-out, it must be transformed into a consonance, a bearer of a triad that admits of composing-out. So transformed, it can unfold with its own passing tones. Harmonically, however, the thus elaborated triad has no relationship to the point of origin of the passing tone. Thus, in example 88, the *C* triad derives its logical justification from the passing *e*, or the passing sixth *e–c*. (See section 4.)

Thus counterpoint teaches us to hear correctly: it teaches us what is to be heard horizontally and what vertically. Not every vertical combination of tones can be heard as a true vertical combination.[14] How inartistic it would be to try, for example, to read the *e, f♯, a, b* in the Bach *E*-minor Prelude cited above [in example 84] as a chord!

Although the last example may be convincing, the situation becomes more difficult when the dissonance is made independent [by being given consonant support] in such a way that no [dissonant] simultaneity exists on the surface. It was the capacity for distance-hearing *(Fernhören)*—the masters' ability to retain aurally the point of departure even when indulging in the freedom of triadic unfolding—that was the hallmark of their genius. Thus Beethoven, to return again to example 88, even lends the composing-out of the *C* sound a motivic character; but in spite of its local enhancement, he does not forget to lead it forward as a mere passing event. This procedure might be compared with that of a drama in which the poet, in spite of any number of intervening monologues, must never lose the thread of the action.

To the possibility that we have discussed so far of having a dissonant passing tone appear as a consonance, a new one may now be added. The former procedure is to be understood as follows: two passing tones, consonant with each other, would have formed dissonances with a bass note; this bass note, however, was omitted. The voice that thereby came to appear in the lowest position was really an *inner voice* (see example 89a) or, which comes to the same thing, the bass itself moved as a passing tone into an inner voice; in this manner the lower voice unfolds the lower space, the lower third of the triad, while the upper voice simultaneously unfolds the upper (see b).

---

13. Here we see a process exactly opposite to that described by the usual harmony treatise. The latter always presents the $\frac{6}{3}$ chord as inversion of a triad, while here we find that the root position is derived from the $\frac{6}{3}$. See Schenker, *Free Composition*, "Addition of a Root," p. 90.

[14. In this context the somewhat cryptic "true vertical combination" *(wirkliches Uebereinander)* might best be interpreted as "harmonically derived (or motivated) vertical combination." Cf. chap. 1, footnote 19.]

Example 89.

Let us now consider the following situation (*Kontrapunkt II*, p. 182):

Example 90.

We see in the first bar of the upper voice an essentially dissonant passing tone moving from *f* to *d* by way of *e*. At the same time the inner voice leaps to *a*, the fifth, a tone *consonant* with the cantus firmus and also consonant—again as a fifth—with the upper voice. There arises here the very peculiar effect that the relationship of the two upper voices, the half notes, penetrates more conspicuously into the foreground than does the relation of middle voice to lower voice. The dissonant passing tone is so strong that it virtually forces the middle voice into its domain. And where does this originate? It is only because upper and middle voices are elevated to the status of an internally consonant setting that the dissonance, the passing tone, achieves independence and a life of its own. Because the motion of the inner voice primarily serves the passing tone and is weaker in relation to the lowest voice, this type of progression is called a "leaping passing tone" (*springender Durchgang*). Let us now imagine that the lower voice itself leaps to *a* of the middle voice and then returns to *d:*

Example 91.

In this case we recognize at once in the motion of the lower voice the phenomenon that we earlier called *divider* (see chapter 2, section 2). Or if we expand example 76 by adding to the upper arpeggiation the passing tone *d*, then we understand the profound meaning of this very common bass arpeggiation as a leap, by the bass, to the inner voice; the arpeggiation literally *captures* the dissonant passing tone, makes it consonant, and thereby enables it to achieve *independent chordal unfolding*. The model of the divider (example 91) represents a *primal movement:* in the lower voice, the simplest arpeggiation, equivalent to I—V—I (the first harmonic event); in the upper, the first passing tone of diatony (the first voice-leading event).

2.   The Linear Progressions

> Anyone who has not heard music in terms of such linear progressions
> simply has never heard it!
>
> Schenker, *Jahrbuch I*

By *linear progression (Auskomponierungszug)* Schenker means the compositional unfolding of a specific[15] interval, one of the intervals of the chord of nature:
the fifth and third, as well as their respective inversions, the fourth and sixth.
Additional possibilities include inverting the step of a second into a seventh, which
signifies an ascending or descending register transfer[16] of the second and therefore
an enlargement of its space; and the octave, which also amounts to a register
transfer, in this case of the same tone. The hallmark of the linear progression
is the *passing tone.*[17] "The linear progression always presupposes a passing tone;
there is no linear progression without a passing tone and no passing tone without

---

15.   The criterion of specificity, and thus of precision, cannot be met by the vague "linear
concept" of Kurth's, in response to which Schenker has written:

> Motion in music is more than simply motion *per se:* it is a precisely delimited
> motion. The precision of the motion derives from the fact that the motion in
> each case fills in a precisely defined triad. The precise definition of the triad
> is given us by nature; as a result, the decisive precision of that motion which
> in particular is the content of music issues from the specific triad of nature,
> which is vertical in form and therefore knows nothing of the fourth. Music
> was elevated from its initially aimless flowing movement to an art only by a
> deliberately chosen motion maintained within definite limits in an artistically
> conscious way. (*Jahrbuch I*, p. 95.)

At the same time, Schenker accordingly does away with the concept of "sequence" so
favored by conventional theory:

> The concept of passing motion imposes as a first duty the establishment of
> its point of departure and goal *(Anfangs- und Endpunkt);* no one may speak
> of a passing motion who cannot accurately specify both, any more than one
> could speak of a passage-way between two streets without knowing which
> streets are connected by it. The word "sequence," which rolls so glibly off
> the tongue when one is unable to explain certain passing motions fully, is unjusti-
> fiable. The mere fact that theory is able to coin such a term is no proof of its
> aptness. (*Jahrbuch II*, p. 86.)

[16. See *Free Composition*, pp. 51–52 and p. 85.]

[17. *Durchgang*, literally, "that which passes through." The term requires flexibility
in translation, and I have rendered it elsewhere in this volume as "passing motion," which
can mean either one or several passing tones. In some contexts *Durchgang* still more
generally denotes one or more transient event(s) of various or mixed categories, but in
connection with the topic of linear progressions it is usually best interpreted as the very
specific "passing tone," with its implication of stepwise origin and continuation.]

a linear progression."[18] The linear progression represents an extension of strict counterpoint's fundamental law that assigns a passing character to the dissonance. Free composition is [thus] revealed as a *prolongation* of strict counterpoint.

Before we turn to a discussion of the individual linear progressions, the following excerpt from Schenker's *Kontrapunkt* should be quoted toward amplification of the passing-tone concept, which is the essential component of the linear progression:

> If the motion into the second half note [in an upper voice] introduces a dissonance, there exists on the weak beat, strictly speaking, only an interval whose upper tone is dissonant against the lower voice; at the same time, the second interval still remains under the influence of the harmony of the immediately preceding strong beat. It is as though the harmony of the strong beat were still present at the weak beat—as if it were still sounding:

Example 92.

This effect is present in both cases [a and b of example 92], but in the case of a passing tone in the lower voice (see b), it is, moreover, prolonged and intensified in a special way: inasmuch as at a the lower tone continues through, the very fact of its continuation prolongs in one's memory the sound of the consonant first interval, and all the more clearly so because all intervallic definitions are based on the lowest voice. In the second case (at b), however, the lower voice gives up the means to do what it was above all obliged to do, namely, to provide an audible continuation of the harmony established on the strong beat; therefore it is particularly necessary in this case to retain the harmony of the strong beat at least in memory. If, for the sake of greater clarity, we write the tone (at b) to be prolonged in a lower register—since it is *purely imaginary (geistig)* in nature—:

Example 93.

---

18. Schenker, *Jahrbuch II*, p. 24. [This is one of the most potent and compelling of Schenker's observations. Its first part—"no linear progression without a passing tone"—is obvious, an analytic statement once the definition of "linear progression" is understood; but the consequent—"no passing tone without a linear progression"—, understood in its ramifications, is a revelation that entails Schenker's theory of composing-out and of structural strata as surely as a theorem of Euclidean geometry is entailed by its premises.]

then we gain an insight into the true [. . .] nature of the lower voice [in free composition] and how, in relation to the scale degree to be imagined even lower, it actually takes on the meaning of another upper voice. In other words, it is precisely the dissonant passing tone that confirms the harmony of the strong beat more reliably and emphatically than the consonant weak beat, which, as we saw earlier, does not imply a unity of harmonic effect [within the bar] and often leads even to a more or less explicit change of harmony.

Alongside all of the physicality (which is always to be understood as independent) of the possible intervals in strict counterpoint, with the first appearance of the dissonant passing tone there arises a curious intrusion of the imaginary: it consists in the covert retention, by the ear, of the consonant point of departure that accompanies the dissonant passing tone on its journey. It is as though the dissonance would always carry along with it the impression of its consonant origin, and thus we comprehend in the deepest sense the stipulation of strict counterpoint, which demands of the dissonant passing tone that it proceed only by the step of a second and only in the same direction [as that by which it was introduced].[19]

The implications of this effect are of great importance: we recognize in the dissonant passing tone the most dependable—indeed the only—vehicle of melodic content. While in first species the melodic line still unfolds laboriously, chord by chord, in second species we see it move ahead within the framework of a sustaining vertical sonority. Therefore even two-voice counterpoint shows the beginnings of melodic *composing-out*—that is, the *simultaneous development of the same single harmony in both vertical and horizontal directions*—to the extent that it is capable of setting up a relationship of strong beat and weak beat such that both express the same harmony. When the weak beat is consonant, this relationship of strong and weak beats may or may not be present, according to the particular interval; but it is always present when the weak beat is dissonant.[20]

Schenker names linear progressions after the respective intervals that they traverse. The linear progression can either descend or ascend. It guarantees coherence, and establishes it even when the foreground admits apparent deviations. An example of a descending third-progression is provided by the passage cited earlier from Mozart's A-Major Sonata, K. 331 (examples 17 and 18).[21] The connection established by the linear progression enables us to understand the enlargement of the second repetition. Example 87 (on Beethoven, op. 106) shows an ascending third-progression.

----

19. "The dissonance introduced by step on the weak beat must continue in the same direction as that by which it arrived." Schenker, *Kontrapunkt I*, p. 240.

20. Schenker, *Kontrapunkt II*, pp. 58–59.

[21. The third-progression is expressed by the tones e^2 (bar 1), d^2 (bar 2), $c\#^2$ (bar 4).]

a.   The Third-Progression

The first four bars of Chopin's Nocturne in $E\flat$, op. 9 no. 2, provide another example of a third-progression:

Example 94.   Chopin, Nocturne in E♭ Major, op. 9 no. 2

Represented as simply as possible, the meaning is this:

Example 95.

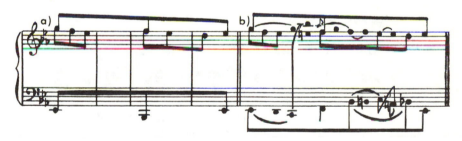

The illustration not only reveals the third-progression that extends over the whole passage, but also shows how offshoots from each of its [first two] tones project into the inner voice (a).[22] Regarding the exchange of voices in bar 2, see

---

[22. Schenker often calls such offshoots *Innenterzzüge*, interior third-progressions.]

section 5.²³ This structure is clarified also by Chopin's correct placement of the bar lines.²⁴

Example 88 shows a third-progression in which the lower voice leads.²⁵ As explained above, *d* rises to *f* by way of the passing tone *e*. Compare also the third-progression [*e–f♯–g*, in the bass] in example 84. Examples to be cited later in connection with the concept of fundamental structure *(Ursatz)* will show how a third-progression, in extended form, can provide an adequate framework for an entire piece.

[23. Jonas uses the term *Stimmentausch* (exchange of voices) somewhat freely. Its meaning is this: the g^2 of bar 1 moves to f^2 in bar 3, while *C* of the bass is shifted upward (see the arrow) to produce the bb^2 that leads to ab^2; thus the two voices have exchanged their respective functions as upper voice and inner voice. This is not voice-exchange in Schenker's technical sense, but instead represents *reaching over* (see p. 106.) The stems and other interpretative graphics in the bass staff of b) have been added by the editor.]

24. See above, chap. 1, section 3. Compare also the discussion of Mozart's Sonata in *A* Major, K. 331. A further observation may be offered here: In a third-progression distributed over a four-bar phrase, if each tone of the progression is itself composed-out in agreement with the meter, one of the unfoldings—usually the last—logically must be expanded. This applies to the example from Mozart's *A*-Major Sonata (examples 17 and 18) as well as to example 6 from Beethoven's Sonata op. 110; in the latter, the third third-arpeggiation *eb–c* is expanded into a third-progression by means of *db*. Or, consider the following example from the second theme of Mozart's Sonata in *F*, K. 332:

Example 96.   Mozart, Sonata in F Major, K. 332

The third third, *c–e*, is expanded by a passing *d*. [The interpretation of g^2 in the example as the first main upper-voice tone is determined by the larger context of this passage in the sonata. Lacking this particular context, the passage might be interpreted differently.] This dissonant passing tone is then made consonant by the divider [*g*], a leaping passing tone in the bass.

The following remarks by Schenker are apposite: "The first stepwise motions of second-species counterpoint in two and three voices already exhibit the third-progression. There, the articulation of this linear progression as a unified whole is secured by the single cantus-firmus tone. But even in free composition, the possible transformation by prolongation of its middle tone—the dissonant passing tone—into a consonance does not negate the unity of the third-progression." *(Jahrbuch I*, p. 192.)

[25. See p. 84ff.; also fn. 42.]

b. The Fifth-Progression

A larger segment of the diatonic system is presented in the fifth-progression. Like the third-progression, it can extend over merely part of a totality, as in:[26]

Example 97a. Mozart, Sonata in Bb Major, K. 333

Schubert's Quartet in *A* Minor, op. 29, bar 23ff., provides an example of a fifth-progression in which the first passing tone is expanded through an arpeggiation of its own which has a motivic character and even represents an enlargement.

[26. The example is somewhat oversimplified. The tones c^2 and bb^1 in bars 5 and 6 (repeated in bars 7–8) are part of a subordinate motion that prolongs, by voice exchange, the d^2 of bar 4. (One reason for this is that bars 4–6 are based merely on a 10–6–6 outer-voice counterpoint, in contrast to the stronger cadential bass of bars 1–4.) After the digression of bars 5–8, the third of the *Bb* triad (which is the third tone of the governing fifth-progression) is regained in bar 9, but in a higher register as d^3. (The tones f^3–eb^3–d^3 of bars 8–9 recapitulate, in the high register, the first segment of the fifth-progression from bars 1–4.) The small interior third-progression c–bb–a within bar 9 parallels that of bars 4–6 (d–c–bb).]

Example 97b. Schubert, String Quartet in A Minor, D. 804

The first arpeggiation, e^2–$c\sharp^2$–a^1, finds a parallel in the arpeggiation a^2–$f\sharp^2$–d^2, whose tones are preceded by accented passing tones or appoggiaturas (see section 3). The head-tone (see below, g) e^2 is regained in bar 30 [as an appoggiatura to the passing d^2, the second tone of the fifth-progression]. The motion of bars 28–29 leads first to the inner-voice tone $c\sharp^2$, which is immediately restated as a short appoggiatura. Observe the marvellous parallelism of this small constellation of appoggiaturas, the third $c\sharp^2$–e^2, to the third e^2–$g\sharp^2$ leading into bar 27; these appoggiaturas relate specifically to the tones of the arpeggiation. How clearly Schubert underscores this arpeggiation through the dynamic markings:

bar 25/26   27   30

⟨ < > ⟩ f > decr. p fp

a^2 $f\sharp^2$ d^2

The fifth-progression can also provide cohesion over the span of an entire work, as here:

Example 98.   Bach, *WTC I,* Prelude in B♭ Major

(See also chapter 4, on fundamental structure.)

The fifth-progression can, of course, also ascend. Ascending progressions, incidentally, are to be understood as if the tone toward which the progression is directed—in this case the fifth—were implied in advance (by virtue of our inborn sense of the overtone series) and "fetched," so to speak, from below by an inner voice.[27]

Example 99.   Handel, Suite in B♭ Major, Aria

In the bass the rising fifth-progression takes on special significance because of the frequent occurrence of motion to the upper fifth as divider; it is natural in such cases to expand the motion to the fifth by means of passing tones.[28]

---

27. See Schenker, *Free Composition,* pp. 45–46. Regarding example 99, see Schenker, *Der Tonwille,* IV. Jahrgang, Heft 2/3 (April/Sept. 1924), p. 3ff.

[28. See Schenker, *Free Composition,* p. 29 and fig. 14.]

Example 100. Bach, Prelude in C Major, BWV 924

The same thing applies to the falling fifth, whether it represents a return from the divider to the fundamental (V—I) or a motion to the fifth below (I—IV).

Example 101. Mozart, Sonata in A Minor, K. 310, Third Movement, Bars 87–95

The fifth-progression is often formally divided at the third, its point of internal articulation.[29] With respect to an ascending fifth-progression in the bass, we have already encountered such an articulation in connection with the arpeggiation I—III—V (especially in minor). Generally speaking, this segmentation assumes special significance for form. Here we might call attention once again to the examples from Beethoven mentioned earlier: opp. 97, 106, and 125. A special example is Mozart's *Requiem*, at the connection from "Oro supplex" to the "Lacrymosa":

[29. See example 97 and the accompanying footnote. In that excerpt the segmentation is supported by the use of two cadential progressions in the bass, one for each of the two segments. Refer also to Schenker, *Free Composition*, p. 34 and figs. 19–20.]

Example 102.   Mozart, *Requiem*, K. 626

The bass, departing from the *A* harmony, moves first to *f* through *ab*, *g*, and (implicitly) *f♯*, with a tonicization of each tone. Only then does it continue through *e* to the *d* at "Lacrymosa." The ascending fifth-progressions *f–ab–bb–c* in Chopin's *f*-minor Ballade, which includes composing-out even of the passing tone *bb* (first in bars 16–22, then, extended, in bars 31–57!), should also be examined.

c. The Fourth-Progression

The fourth-progression occurs often in the upper voice when, having begun on the fifth of the triad, it descends by step in conjunction with a half-cadence in the lower voice:[30]

Example 103a.   C. P. E. Bach, Sonata in G Major, Wq. 56 no. 2

a)

[30. Regarding the first example, the *d* in the last half of bar 2 can hardly represent a principal tone in the upper voice. The first two bars rather express an ascent to *b* ($\hat{3}$), which moves to *a* over V in bar 8. The upper voice might be represented graphically as follows:

The third *c–a* in bar 2 is answered by *b–g* (see the brackets), inverted to a rising sixth in order to introduce the higher pitch level of the consequent phrase. In bars 5ff., the upper voice follows the bass in parallel tenths.]

Example 103b.   C. P. E. Bach, Rondo in A Minor, Wq. 56 no. 5

Example 104.   Beethoven, Sonata in E♭ Major, op. 31 no. 3, Menuetto

Usually a repetition follows in which the fourth-progression is extended to a fifth in order to reach a closure. This is significant with respect to the nature of two-part form.[31] See also g in this section, "The Head-Tone of the Linear Progression." Schenker symbolizes the stepwise descent within the diatonic system by $\hat{5}$—$\hat{4}$—$\hat{3}$—$\hat{2}$—$\hat{1}$.

---

31. Antecedent-consequent construction. Regarding "interruption," consult Schenker, *Free Composition*, pp. 36–40.

Everything that applies to a fifth-progression in the bass applies also to a fourth-progression, with, of course, an exchange of functions—that is, the descending fourth represents development, and the ascending one return. Whoever has understood the nature of these fourth-progressions and their significance for coherence will be able to add many examples to those cited here.[32]

Example 105.   Bach, Violin Partita in D Minor, BWV 1004, Chaconne

Example 106.   Beethoven, Symphony V, Scherzo (after Schenker, *Der Tonwille VI*)

The [descending] path to the dominant is so strongly rooted in our consciousness that when the bass begins a descent from the fundamental, the maximum opportunity to generate tension by means of expansion is open to the composer. The release of such tension can even become the content of an entire piece. Thus Mozart, in his *C*-minor Fantasy, K. 475, clearly attempts [at the beginning] to establish a descending fourth-progression *C—G*. This progression is interrupted when it reaches *Ab*; the course is changed abruptly to return to *B*, from which it again descends, moving beyond *G* to *Gb* (*F♯*). The *G* that arrives in bar 18 is now heard as only an auxiliary-note belonging to *F♯*. Not until the repetition, near the end *(Tempo primo)*, of the first part does the bass arrive at *G* as the dominant of *C*. In this way the plan for an entire composition—the plan of this Fantasy—grows out of the sense of tonal space, the obligation set up by the composing-out of a fourth-progression.[33] Only their sense of tonal space can explain the masters' powers of improvisation, and also their accuracy with respect to the overall plan of their works. Their ear hears the thread of the linear progression through all details of compositional unfolding and over distances of any magnitude. How subtly Chopin, in his Fantasy op. 49, extends the fourth-progression of the first two bars from the *poco a poco doppio movimento* after the first double bar up to the *agitato:*

---

32. Example 106: after Schenker, *"Beethoven: V. Sinfonie (Schluss),"* *Der Tonwille* *VI* (1923), p. 9.

[33. For a fuller discussion of this piece see Jonas, "Improvisation in Mozart's Klavierwerken," *Mozart Jahrbuch 1967* (Salzburg, 1968), pp. 179–181.]

Example 107.   Chopin, Fantasy op. 49

Or, consider the path of the bass:

Example 108.   Chopin, Fantasy op. 49

Chopin, with his secure sense of tonal space, is able to extend the *Gb*; how confidently he elaborates, in the *lento, sostenuto,* the *B(Cb)* triad, with no fear of losing coherence. Also of importance is the fact that the master underscores these interconnections by remaining in the same register. For further clarification a small example from Chopin's Mazurka op. 56 no. 2 may be cited. In the *a*-minor section, where the bass moves through a rising fifth-progression, Chopin writes as follows:

Example 109. Chopin, Mazurka op. 56 no. 2

It is clear that the octave C connects back to the octave B, and at the arrival of E, where the bass again takes over the motivic unfolding, the low E is given its due at least by the appoggiatura.[34]

A discussion of the following example from Mozart's Piano Sonata in F major, K. 332, is postponed until chapter 4, section 3.[35]

Example 110. Mozart, Sonata in F Major, K. 332

On the topic of the rising fourth-progression, the following observations should be made. If the bass ascends by step from G as the fifth of the key [i.e., the dominant], and if each of the passing tones is elaborated, the question arises what should happen at the last passing tone B, which is supposed to carry us forward directly to C. Leaving aside the fact that the V—I effect with an explicit fifth- or fourth-leap in the bass is necessary especially at the cadence, whenever the B is not composed out as a B triad, the G harmony appears in $\frac{6}{3}$ position before the cadence. Moreover, in rising by step from G, the tones G—B are grouped by the ear as a third, so that the rising fourth-progression in the bass is not heard, as it is in the upper voice, as an unfolding of a segment of the C sound, but rather as follows:

[34. Consult also Ernst Oster, "Register and the Large-Scale Connection," rpt. in M. Yeston, ed., *Readings in Schenker Analysis and Other Approaches* (New Haven: Yale University Press, 1976).]

[35. This example, like the preceding one, belongs to the digression into matters of register rather than to the presentation of the fourth-progression.]

Example 111.

Let us consider example 72. The bass climbs from *G♯* as V in c minor, first to *A♯*. From there it moves via *F𝄪*, the third of the *D♯* triad, to *D♯* and thence back again to *G♯* before the eventual cadence to *C♯*. Such a motion as this one from *G♯* to *A♯* is usually termed a deceptive cadence (V—VI). (See above, chapter 1, section 5.) The psychology of the deceptive cadence, however, seems to me to be that of the formation in example 111. This illustrates the attempt to move by step through the fourth and arrive at the fundamental. Since this course would necessarily carry the bass into the leading tone, however, the bass stops at the first passing tone (VI) and seeks its way to the fifth once again. This new path leads through II, at which point the first passing tone [scale degree 6̂] remains in place as an upper or inner voice, to move on to the third of V, the leading tone. In the Bach example, therefore, as follows:

Example 112. Bach, *WTC I,* Prelude in C♯ Minor

In the *Pastoral* Symphony, Beethoven connects the third movement to the fourth by the expansion of a fourth-progression. At the end of the "Lustiges Zusammensein der Landleute" the bass moves from *C* not directly to the *F* expected on the basis of the preceding measures, but first to *D♭*—the beginning of "Gewitter, Sturm"—, so as to arrive at *F* only through chromatic passing tones. (At this point, *ff* and full orchestra except for piccolo.)

Example 113. Beethoven, Symphony VI

How well the tension suits the intended effect of the approaching storm. This tension is brought about not by any external means, but by an intrinsically musical procedure. But this is possible only because we expect the *F* both for reasons intrinsic to us and for reasons having to do with association.[36]

[36. That is, the association with the falling fifth *C—F* shown in the first two bars of example 113.]

The pre-established course of a fourth-progression—here a descending one—enables Brahms to connect two formal sections with each other in the following example:

Example 114. Brahms, Waltz op. 39 no. 14

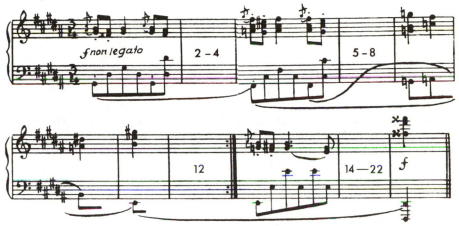

Brahms places the formal division just at the *E*, and, with secure awareness of the linear progression, even sets it with a minor triad. How could one understand this with an explanation that assumed "modulations" to *f♯* minor, *G* major, *e* minor, etc.? The unity of the piece and its formation resides only in the fourth-progression.

d. The Sixth-Progression

The sixth-progression represents an expansion, by means of inversion, of the motion to the third. The passage cited earlier from Mozart's Quartet in *C*, K. 465, in reference to arpeggiation (example 64) may serve as an example. The arpeggiation is filled in to form a linear progression; a sketch of the voice leading is provided in example 115.[37]

Example 115.   Mozart, String Quartet in C Major, K. 465

[37. See also *Free Composition*, fig. 99, 3, and the explanation on p. 82 of the same. Further clarification of the dissonances in this famous opening is given by Jonas in Schenker's *Harmony*, p. 346.]

e. The Seventh-Progression

Even the motion to a passing tone—a second—can be elongated by inversion. The resulting seventh-progression, of course, counts only as an upward or downward register transfer of the passing second. Let us return for a moment to the Prelude in *C* major (BWV 924) by Bach (see example 100). In bar 3, a purely mechanical continuation would have led the bass to *g* at the second quarter. Instead, it leaps to e^1; as a result, it cannot proceed directly to *f* in the next bar. Rather, it descends gradually from e^1 to *f:* instead of the second, *e–f,* it moves through the seventh e^1–*f.* Who could doubt that the events between e^1 and *f* count as merely passing phenomena? The cause of this inversion lies in the top voice, which connects g^2 to a^1; the bass joins this movement in parallel counterpoint. Clearly, the seventh-space itself is in turn organized and subdivided—into thirds, which take on the aspect of independent chords. This is achieved by the following voice leading:[38]

Example 116.   Bach, *WTC I,* Prelude in C Major, BWV 924

Concerning the fifths at the beginning of each measure and their avoidance by means of interpolated sixths, see below, section 7. Of special interest here is the unity of the linear progression and its subdivision by thirds, and also the manifestation, through the chromatic tones, of the tonicization principle, which breathes life into the individual triads. The opening of the Prelude in *Bb* from Bach's *Well-Tempered Clavier,* Book I, may serve as an example of a downward register transfer that uses arpeggiation within a seventh:[39]

Example 117.   Bach, *WTC I,* Prelude in Bb Major

---

38. See Schenker, *Der Tonwille IV* (1923), p. 4.
39. Observe in bar 2 the suspension *d* above the bass note *c,* which points up the end of the linear progression.

Recall also the expansion of a third-progression in Beethoven's Sonata op. 90 (example 4) by the initial attempt to invert the progression of a second, *g–f♯*. Consider also Schubert's Waltz op. 9 no. 36:

Example 118. Schubert, Waltz op. 9 no. 36

Here the ascending fifth-progression *F—c* is expanded by the seventh-progression *f—G*. How such a seventh-progression can effect unification over the longest spans may be shown by Schenker's illustration[40] of the Prelude of Bach's Partita III in *E* for Violin:

Example 119. Bach, Partita for Violin in E, Prelude (after Schenker, *Jahrbuch I*)

---

40. From *Jahrbuch I*, p. 75.

f. The Octave-Progression

The octave-progression likewise amounts to an ascending or descending register transfer—in this case, of a single tone. This tone is carried through a complete octave by means of a motion through passing tones. What a distance stands between the first, simplest octave-arpeggiation and the spacious octave-progression in Bach's *C*-Major Prelude of the *Well-Tempered Clavier*, Book I:

Example 120.   Bach, *WTC I,* Prelude in C Major (after Schenker, *Five Graphic Musical Analyses*)

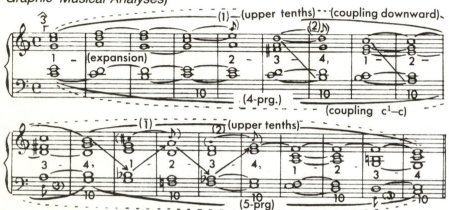

Example 120 is taken from Schenker's *Five Graphic Musical Analyses*[41] so far as necessary for our purpose. It shows the counterpoint in parallel tenths that accompanies the passing tones, and also the subdivision of the octave into a fourth- and a fifth-progression.[42] The concept of coupling applies here as well, in reference to the connection c^1–c.[43]

---

41. Second edition, with an introduction by Felix Salzer (New York: Dover Publications, 1969).

[42. It is significant that the designations "fourth-progression" and "fifth-progression" apply specifically to the bass, while the corresponding segments in the upper voice are designated "upper tenth." This is because the bass is seen as the *leading voice* by virtue of its delineation of the *C* sonority. The stepwise progressions of the upper voice do not count as linear progressions in the same strong sense as do those of the bass: they represent secondary stepwise motions that result from the upper voice's fixed intervallic relationship of parallel tenths with the bass. See Schenker, *Free Composition*, p. 78ff., and below, especially p. 84ff.]

43. In *Jahrbuch II*, p. 14, Schenker writes, "Observe here, too, the connection of different registers through octave coupling. In appearance an idle interplay of rising and falling, falling and rising, octave coupling has as its true purpose to generate content, to connect high and low registers and maintain their distinct identities; but in all cases—and this is what must be emphasized—it signifies an inner tension and promotes coherence of formal parts, and not infrequently of a whole work." And, in *Jahrbuch I*, p. 69, "For a deeper grasp of form, the technique of registral (octave) couplings is of importance. I conceive

The arrows in bars 12–15 indicate the true path of the upper voice, which in places is carried through by an inner voice—for example, the continuation of b^1 to bb, etc. In bars 12–15, $c\sharp^2$–d^2 and b^1–c^2 are superposed inner voices and correspond to a^2 and g^2 in bars 5 and 7. The parallelism is particularly wonderful following immediately, as it does, the formal subdivision at the dominant. This subdivision is strengthened, moreover, by the addition of the bass note d[44] in bar 10, which is paralleled by G in bar 18.

The clearest proof that Bach had in mind first of all the linear progression, without the decoration of the superposed inner voices, is handed down to us in the first version of the prelude.[45] It is clear there that bars 5 and 7 were inserted later; and in bar 12, bb^1 still appears in the upper voice and $c\sharp^1$ in the inner voice!

This much must be said: those who fail to hear the unity of this voice-leading progression, but instead feel their way laboriously sound by sound, hearing only a concatenation of "chords," will miss the most characteristic element of the synthesis; they do not experience the true coherence.

Although we regard division of the octave at the fifth, producing a fourth- and a fifth-progression, as the natural division, it is also possible to secure unity in an octave-progression even in case of a less natural division. This can be accomplished using the major third, or, more exactly, three major thirds, in which case the octave tone can be reached only through an enharmonic change:

Example 121.

Here it is true that the principle of the fifth is lacking; yet the octave can nonetheless guarantee unity for a section of a composition. This case could be considered to lie at the boundary of tonality.

g. The Conjunction and Alignment of Linear Progressions

After the discovery of individual linear progressions, the question arises how they can interact and be interconnected. Strict counterpoint offers instruction here as well:

> The concept of nodal point, which plays such a large role in free composition, should be considered first of all in connection with dissonant passing tones.

---

the horizontal unwinding of an octave as a prolongation of the notion of direct octave coupling. The octave coupling defines a structural unit that prevents the ear from going astray. That is its value for formal considerations." See also *Free Composition*, p. 52 and pp. 85–86.

44. See example 88a and Schenker, *Free Composition*, p. 90.

45. In the *Clavierbüchlein vor Wilhelm Friedemann Bach* (1720). [Facsimile edition, ed. by Ralph Kirkpatrick, New Haven: Yale University Press, 1959.]

By virtue of its motion through a third, the dissonant passing tone gives the two consonant points the significance of beginning and end of a third-space that is to be perceived as a unit; at the same time it releases the concluding tone for service as the initial tone of a new tonal event which attaches to the end of the preceding one:[46]

Example 122.

If we imagine a fourth-progression in place of the fourth-leap in the second bar, we see clearly the conjunction of two linear progressions. Refer to example 103, the G-Major sonata by C. P. E. Bach; d^2 as end-point of the rising third-progression simultaneously becomes the initial tone of the descending fourth-progression.

One further concept needs to be discussed here. Under the title "On the Head-Tone of the Linear Progression" in *Jahrbuch II*, p. 15, Schenker explains that

> Descending linear progressions in the upper voice signify a motion to an inner voice of the same or a subsequent chord, and ascending ones a motion from inner to upper voice. Thus the [implicitly] retained head-tone of a falling linear progression maintains the real register of the upper voice; that of a rising progression becomes an inner voice:

> To continue the content, it suffices to pick up the head-tone of a descending linear progression once more, as if no linear progression had intervened.

Ultimately, then, example 103 is to be understood as follows:

Example 123.

The same applies [with appropriate modification] to example 99 [and example 104].

All voice leading, insofar as it is to have meaning and coherence, must serve the unfolding and elaboration of a triad. Every horizontal motion, every linear

---

46. Schenker, *Kontrapunkt II*, p. 59.

progression, stands for a vertical interval conception. The composing out [of such vertical conceptions] constitutes music. From this standpoint it is idle to speak of polyphony versus homophony. The contrapuntal basis of a Bach fugue is no different from that of a Mozart sonata or a Schubert song. The conduct of the voices is always governed by that contrapuntal basis and by the triad for which those voices speak. Indeed, the theme of a Bach fugue, in spite of its apparently monophonic character, contains a complete contrapuntal structure. Schenker's discussion of the theme of the *B*-Major Fugue from *WTC II* (in a polemic against the "linear" hearing and interpretation by Ernest Kurth[47]) may illustrate how the tones of the theme literally pervade all planes of the triad and thus continuously connect lower, middle, and upper voices:

Example 124a.   Bach, *WTC II,* Fugue in B Major, Theme

Against Kurth's interpretation I place my own:

Example 124b.

Here we find a realization of the *B*-major triad (see 1.). In this instance it pleases Bach to carry through the unfolding by means of an obligato three-voice counterpoint, as shown at 2. The upper voice fills the fourth-space from *f♯* to *b* within the harmony—this fourth-space is completely definite, a higher-level unit of voice-leading that subsumes also Kurth's concept of "leading-tone tension"—and the lower voice moves through the third-progression *B*–*d♯*. Because of the parallel motion of the two linear progressions, the danger of parallel fifths arises; in order to align the four tones of the fourth-progression with the three of the third-progression, and to avoid the 5–5 succession, a 5–6 alternation is used. Is my explanation not simpler than Kurth's? Does it not reveal the theme's origin more clearly and present the composing out (the melodic movement—see 3.) more convincingly? True, it may appear to Kurth more difficult than his own vague ideas—but would that by itself dispute the superior simplicity of my interpretation? I am aware that to speak of third-, fourth-, and fifth-progressions may at first intimidate, only because those voice-leading units oblige the ear to definiteness, and allow feeling to enter only after the ear has learned to hear. I say "at first," but I really doubt that this can ever change.[48]

[47. In *Grundlagen des linearen Kontrapunkts,* p. 45.]
48. *Jahrbuch I,* p. 97.

Also bound to the concept of retention of the head-tone[49] is a certain type of formal organization. Two-part form was mentioned in connection with examples 103 and 104; it was explained how, in the repetition, the fourth-progression is extended to a conclusive fifth-progression. This is possible only because the fourth-progression's point of origin is to be thought of as retained, making possible an immediate connection with the fifth-progression.

We see again the importance of the *a priori* awareness of the intervals within our ear. It enables the ear to hold fast to the point of origin and to bestow coherence over the physically manifest sounds. Antecedent-consequent construction owes its existence to our ability to retain the head-tone. Consider the first eight bars of Mozart's *A*-Major Sonata, K. 331 (see example 17), and observe with eye and ear that the resumption in bar 5 [of the beginning] rests not on the motivic alone, but, essentially, on the act of once again laying hold of e^2 as fifth of the *A* triad.

The discussion of the *B*-major fugue subject brings us to another point that requires consideration. How do linear progressions that occur simultaneously in different voices relate to each other? It is a simple matter, of course, when the linear progressions compose-out the same type of interval and run parallel to each other, as in the octave-progressions of upper and lower voices in Bach's *C*-Major Prelude (example 120). But even then only one of the voices will lead—in this case the lower one—and the other will follow in counterpoint.[50] Otherwise there are three possibilities to consider: two linear progressions of equal size in contrary motion, two unequal progressions in contrary motion, and two unequal progressions in the same direction. The first possibility most frequently involves third-progressions:

Example 125.

This procedure is identical to what is called exchange of voices, which will be taken up in section 5. The *e* moves to the lower voice, the *c* to the upper. The consonant combination formed by the dissonant passing tones often gives rise in free composition to expansion into a consonant triadic area.

When linear progressions of different sizes are carried out simultaneously the shorter one usually has to delay, either at its beginning, as in the *B*-Major Fugue, or at another suitable place. In the introduction of Beethoven's String Quartet op. 130, bars 4ff., this is accomplished as follows:

---

49. Compare also example 57.

50. See Schenker, *Free Composition*, p. 78. [Also footnote 42 above.]

Example 126. Beethoven, String Quartet in Bb Major, op. 130, Introduction, bar 4ff.

The descending fourth-progression of the bass is set against the rising fifth of the upper voice:

Example 127.

The alignment of passing tones with each other plays a large role even in the simplest composing-out of intervals. Often the passing tones form vertical combinations that—whether consonant or dissonant—are not to be regarded as independent, but only as products of voice leading. Again it is strict counterpoint that shows the way. As Schenker writes,

> The possibility of a dissonant collision on the weak beat is not limited only to the natural situation, in which the bar as a whole preserves the initial harmony; this liberty can be taken even in conjunction with a change of harmony, in which case, to be sure, the resulting voice leading will be of a more artificial character; for example:

Example 128.

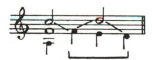

The justification of such a contrapuntal formation, naturally, is given by the passing-tone configuration that reaches from the second to the fourth quarter-note. One can tell from the construction which tone must necessarily appear as the fourth quarter-note, and therefore the second half-note also can easily be heard as relating to that tone even before the fact. Thus the collision on the third quarter is more willingly tolerated the more effortlessly one can recognize its cause in the passing-tone structure.

(The relationship  just described is often particularly effective and useful in deciphering many difficult voice-leading structures in free composition.)[51]

Obviously the *e* merely fills the space between *f* and *d,* and only the latter tones stand in relation to the half-notes and the cantus-firmus tone.

In Bach's music, attractive consonant vertical sounds often arise through rhythmic alteration of passing tones as different passing motions are aligned with each other. The chorales are rich in such configurations. "Es ist das Heil uns kommen her"[52] begins as follows:

Example 129.   Bach, "Es ist das Heil uns kommen her,"
Riemenschneider no. 4

It is based on the following voice leading:

Example 130.

The basic form of the fourth-filling motion in the bass would be as in b. But Bach displaces the eighth-notes, and thus, exactly at the passing dissonant seventh, d^2, of the soprano, there occurs an apparent *D*-major $\frac{6}{3}$ chord, which, however, is by no means to be interpreted harmonically. This proves, again, how senseless it is to isolate vertical sonorities as such, without taking their origins into account. A similar case, to cite only one more example from many, is found in the chorale "Christus, der uns selig macht":

---

51. *Kontrapunkt II,* p. 189.

[52. Erk-Smend numbers in the original captions and references to chorale examples have been changed to the corresponding Riemenschneider numbers, which may be more familiar to American readers.]

Example 131. Bach, "Christus, der uns selig macht,"
Riemenschneider no. 81

In other cases the composing-out process gives rise to dissonant combinations in place of other dissonant ones:[53]

Example 132. Bach, "Herzlich lieb," Riemenschneider no. 107

How superb the effect, at the last quarter of bar 1, of the vertical combination that displaces the one that would normally have occurred there. But it would be completely wrong to speak of a "seventh chord on bb" where instead there is simply an original way of adjusting the composed-out sixth, $eb^2–g^1$, of the upper voice to the fifth, $eb–bb$, of the lower. The next example shows how dissonant combinations may arise through displacement (here for textual reasons) even of parallel passing tones:

Example 133. Brahms, *Fest- und Gedenksprüche,* op. 109 no. 2

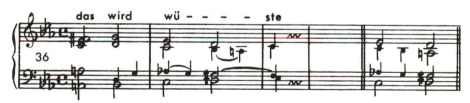

The principle of linear progression unifies motive, phrase, section, and ultimately the total form. It is the organ of coherence.

---

53. See Schenker, *Free Composition,* p. 105.

Example 134.   Bach, *WTC I,* Prelude in C Major (after Schenker, *Five Graphic Musical Analyses*)

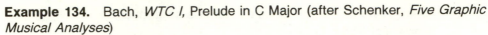

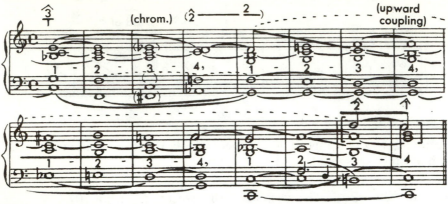

This example is the continuation of example 120. It reveals that the downward octave coupling e^2–e^1 [shown in example 120] is answered by the upward coupling d^1–d^2, with d^2 then moving on to the concluding c^2. Both the descent and the upward arpeggiation are embedded in a higher-level entity, the third-progression e^2–d^2–c^2, which produces coherence for the whole piece.

It should finally be explained why none of our illustrative examples have been taken from newer music. I leave this explanation to Schenker himself, who expresses it clearly in the article "The Art of Improvisation" which opens the first *Jahrbuch:*

> Our generation has laid waste the art of diminution, the composing-out of triads. And, like the fox in the fable, it calls the grapes it cannot reach sour. No longer even able to understand the art of diminution as given to us by the masters in their teaching and their works, it turns mind and ear away from a fundamental law that it is not mature enough to live up to either in creating or in re-creating. It is unaware that all of its uncertainty and weakness, its insatiable desire for the different—different, indeed, from the art of the masters, and even different from the ways of nature—all spring from nothing other than the inability to create horizontal expressions of triadic concepts given by nature.
>
> Our generation therefore banishes its incapability in the pretense of creating novelties, under the proud and telling rubric "progress." (p. 11)

The objection has often been raised against Schenker's theory that it does not come to terms with more recent works and therefore has no validity for them. This is very like rejecting a critique that can distinguish good from bad because it fails to count both as good. In any case, to consider all things of equal validity reflects the trend of our time. It is certainly possible that a narrow range of application might speak against the correctness of a theory. But what if it were the case that a *work* could not stand up under the scrutiny of a *theory?*— a theory about which its author has written, "Because it is derived from the artistic practice of genius, it *is itself art and will remain so;* therefore it can never become 'science'."[54] And further:

> Since this theory is concerned above all with composing-out, with diminution, and therefore demands inventiveness of the creator and artistic sensitivity of the performer and listener, access to it is precluded for those who have no ear for such purely compositional phenomena.[55]

Section 3.   The Remaining Resources for Composing-Out

a.   The Neighboring Tone

If a tone that came about by stepwise motion away from a consonance returns to its point of departure, it produces the configuration of a neighboring tone. While beginning- and end-points are different in the case of a passing tone, with a neighboring tone they are the same:

Example 135.

The passing tone serves the composing-out of an interval; in the case of the neighboring tone, it is as though a tone revolves about its own axis. The neighboring tone thus serves purely as an embellishment. Consequently, the passing-tone concept enjoys a qualitative priority over the neighboring tone. For the ear asks itself: why the display of dissonance if nothing further is entailed? Strict counterpoint, therefore, disallows the dissonant neighboring tone, at least in second species. Since it is precisely strict counterpoint whose task it is to make us aware of the natural and the less natural patterns of voice leading, it is clear that the neighboring tone must yield to the passing tone. Besides, the cantus-firmus tone has too little power to make the formation unambiguous. As soon as we reach third species, where the cantus-firmus tone attains proportionately greater scope, the neighboring tone appears to be better motivated.[56] These cases are especially

---

[54. *Jahrbuch III*, p. 22.]

[55. *Jahrbuch III*, p. 22.]

[56. In *Kontrapunkt* Schenker observes that the most natural placement of the neighboring tone in third species is on the second quarter of the bar, since in that location the neighboring tone (1) is unaccented and (2) returns to its consonant origin above the *same* cantus tone. The least natural placement is the fourth quarter, where the completion of the figure coincides with a new cantus tone. He continues, "when one considers, then, that second-species counterpoint would make available only this less regular variant . . ., one understands still more clearly why the neighboring tone is preferably avoided there" (*II*, p. 76).]

well suited to demonstrate how indispensable the study of counterpoint is for educating the ear.

In free composition we are always kept correctly oriented with regard to the nature of the neighboring tone by means of triadic composing-out. The neighboring tone in free composition may vary in scope from simple melodic embellishment, as it is found even in ornaments, up to the condition of greater independence that results when the bass moves simultaneously, as it often does with a passing tone. In this way the neighboring tone is expanded by being given its own chord. The latter may be dissonant, when the other voices also move to neighboring tones:

Example 136.

(Compare example 103b, C. P. E. Bach, Rondo in *A* Minor, bar 2.)

More important for our considerations are those cases in which the neighboring tone is expanded into a consonant triadic region. This occurs most frequently with the aid of the lower fifth, the so-called *dividing subdominant* I—IV—I.

Example 137.

(Compare example 71.)

Marvelous expansions of a neighboring tone are found in the first and second movements of the *Pastoral* Symphony. The enlargement of bar 11 springs from the seed of the first bar; this ordering of large and small is reversed at the reprise, which is magically conjured forth by the enlargement of this neighboring tone. (See example 138a.) In the second movement the seed of the neighboring tone in the accompanimental figure (in the eighteenth bar before the end) grows into the expansion by first violin and woodwinds; from this the neighboring-tone motion of the flute (as nightingale) develops organically. The neighboring tone still rings through in the basses (third bar from the end) and in the clarinet. (See example 138b.)

Example 138. Beethoven, Sixth Symphony

a)

Another possibility is to let the lower voice remain in place [while the upper moves to a neighboring tone to $\hat{5}$]; the chord produced in this way can be interpreted as VI. If in major a neighboring tone a minor second above the main tone is used, a beautiful mixture results:

Example 139. Mozart, String Quartet in C Major, K. 465, Last Movement, bar 86ff.

(Compare Brahms, Sextet op. 36, in G Major, bars 5ff.)

The lower voice, too, can execute a neighboring motion, perhaps along with a passing tone in the upper voice:

Example 140.

In the development of Schubert's Sonata in *A* Major [D. 959], the bass moves to a lower neighboring tone. (See example 141.) Schenker cites this example in *Harmony* (p. 225); there, admittedly, he still speaks of "modulation." In truth, the example shows a neighboring tone that has been supplied with its own triad, by force of its urge toward tonicality. The chords that immediately precede the *B* triad are needed to avoid the consecutive fifths (see section 6) that would otherwise occur. Observe again how voice-leading phenomena (here the neighboring tone) go hand in hand with harmonic, color-generating phenomena (tonicization):

Example 141.   Schubert, Sonata in A Major, D. 959

The step of a second that produces a neighboring tone can also be inverted to a seventh, and expanded:

Example 142.

A situation that exemplifies this procedure occurs often when a minor triad on the fifth scale degree is converted to major in order to lend it a dominant character. This procedure plays an important role especially in formal sections that have a retransitional purpose *(rückleitende Teile)*. The seventh can be expanded by simple passing tones, or it can be divided into third-segments:

Example 143.   Mozart, String Quartet in D Minor, K. 421, Second Movement

Like the passing tone, the neighboring tone may be of varying magnitude. It may operate overtly or within the motive as an initial expansion; it may govern

a formal section; or, finally, in its maximum extension, it may operate over the course of a whole piece.[57] For free composition, its ornamental character frequently offers an advantage, since with its use *a single point* can be extended!

Example 144. Bach, *WTC I,* Fugue in F Major

b. The Accented Passing Tone and the Suspension[58]

If a passing tone occurs as in 2 of example 145 instead of as in 1,

Example 145.

[57. Although a neighboring tone can be expanded to occupy a very long duration (see example 144 and the reference to it on p. 94), it cannot, according to Schenker's theory of fundamental structure (see chap. 4, and *Free Composition,* p. 42f.), operate literally "over the course of a whole piece." It can embellish a tone of the fundamental line, in which case it will belong to the first stratum of the middleground, but it cannot by itself provide the content of the background, as might be suggested by this formulation.]

[58. *Wechsel- und Vorhaltsnote.* There is no exact English equivalent of *Vorhalt,* which encompasses at least two English terms and several meanings for which no single English word exists. It can mean (1) a regular suspension notated with a tie, thus a literal "holding (-before)"; (2) a weak-strong repetition of a tone that becomes dissonant on the strong beat; or (3) a metrically strong dissonant note that is approached by leap. "Suspension" seems to include at least the notion of preparation, if not also that of explicit tying-over. Meaning (3) is almost accurately captured by "appoggiatura," but this term could suggest a purely ornamental phenomenon of very brief duration (for which the German *Vorschlag* is also used). For example, not everyone would consider "appoggiatura" applicable to the sevenths in example 150. (Yet in a deep sense they are of exactly the same significance as ornamental appoggiaturas, but they are expanded. See *Free Composition,* fig. 110a, we call it an *accented passing tone*. Such a dissonance on the strong beat is not allowed in strict counterpoint, for it would place too great a burden on the cantus-firmus tone. It is precisely strict counterpoint that inculcates an awareness of the different effects of passing tone, accented passing tone, and neighboring tone. It is different in free composition, where composing-out generates larger units and orients us more easily regarding the character of passing tones. For example, in variation 6 of Brahms's *Paganini*-Variations (see example 146),

Example 146. Brahms, *Paganini*-Variations, op. 35, Variation 6

we immediately understand the voice-leading situation, as a direct result of the way the sonorities are composed-out. In the first bar the *B* of the bass is understood as an accented passing tone, and the *b* of the upper voice as a simple passing tone. The special appeal of this passage resides in the fact that at the beginning of the second bar the *E* in the bass makes us expect a change of chord—the bass in the first bar, after all, has completed its composing-out *C–B–A—*; yet at the same time we await the arrival of the main tone *A* in the upper voice, but the latter now takes on the character of an accented passing tone. The tension between rhythmic-motivic aspects and composing-out forms the special character of this variation. Most instructive with regard to all of these phenomena is the study of Chopin's Mazurka in *A* Minor, op. 17 no. 4, with its neighboring and accented passing tones transferred upward from the lower register.[59]

If the dissonance on the strong beat is divested of its passing-tone character,[60] it is called a *suspension*. The suspension can either enter freely or be prepared—that is, be carried over from the preceding bar. Even the fourth species of strict counterpoint introduces to us this prepared form, a type of syncope.[61]

---

example 4, and the discussion on p. 89.) The present subsection deals only very minimally with the *Vorhalt;* each of the three categories mentioned above is treated more fully in the next subsection, *Syncope.* Where *Vorhalt* is used in meaning (3), I have rendered it as *free suspension.*]

[59. . . . *mit ihrem aufgesetzten Nebennoten und Wechselnoten.* This refers, for example, to the neighboring-tone formation $f^2–e^2$ in bars 7–8, in which the neighbor f^2 is transferred upward from an inner voice, and to the accented passing tone c^3 in bar 19, which is also registrally displaced.]

[60. That is, if it enters otherwise than by step.]

61. Also worth mentioning is the *anticipation*—in a sense the opposite of the suspension—, in which a tone that is due to arrive only at a given strong beat appears in advance, on the preceding weak beat.

c. The Syncope

If in strict counterpoint, given a basis of two time-units, a consonant note on the weak beat is continued over to the strong beat, which is specified through connection by means of a tie, a phenomenon known as *syncope* arises.[62]

Example 147.

Here we see for the first time in strict counterpoint the possibility of a dissonance on the strong beat. Although the motion away from a consonant syncope to another consonance is free and may even be by leap, the dissonant syncope must be led *downward by step* to the adjacent consonance:

Example 148.

The *authentic* suspensions[61] are 9–8 and 4–3. In both, no change of harmony occurs on the third beat [i.e., the second weak beat of the suspension formation].

To gain a clear notion of the relationship of strict counterpoint and free composition in respect to the syncope, we must not lose sight of this fact: the element common to the dissonant syncope and the dissonant passing tone is that both occur between two consonances. If this fact is taken together with the syncope's requirement of downward resolution—that is, the necessity of motion in a particular direction, similar to that of the passing tone—it can be understood that the syncope in general represents only a particular form of passing tone:[64]

Example 149.

---

62. Schenker, *Kontrapunkt I*, [p. 331].

[63. *Eigentliche Vorhalte.* See Schenker, *Kontrapunkt II*, p. 84.]

[64. According to this explanation, the syncope formation embodies an *elision;* in example 149, d^2, which would be the consonant point of departure for the passing seventh, is suppressed. There is ample precedent in music theory for the use of elision (or ellipsis) as an explanatory tool. The writings of Heinichen, C. P. E. Bach, and Kirnberger provide many instances. See, for example, George J. Buelow, "Heinichen's Treatment of Disso-

One could perhaps define the difference in this way: with the passing tone, the horizontal motion stands in the foreground, while the syncope implies in a certain way also an emphasis of the vertical relationship. In any case, the syncope always carries with it the *heritage of the passing tone.* If in free composition it may also manifest itself as a free, unprepared suspension (which is there made possible and comprehensible by virtue of composing-out), we nevertheless understand it as a phenomenon that by nature originates in a passing tone—one whose [consonant] point of departure can be regarded as having been elided.

This phenomenon is of fundamental importance for understanding the concept of dissonance in Schenkerian theory. With incredible intuition, Schenker writes in *Kontrapunkt I*, p. 366,

> Thus the *preparation* itself can be elided and the dissonance placed on the strong beat in its absence. *Dissonant* chords thereby arise, for which in certain circumstances a purely *implicit preparation* through the preceding harmony can be assumed; otherwise the apparently free dissonance must be understood as the clearly established internal element of a *latent passing motion.* In the latter case, the elided consonance that would initiate the passing motion is to be inferred from and supplied by the harmony belonging to the dissonance itself. In this way we arrive at the so-called *free suspensions*, and it may be that the ultimate origin of seventh-chords[65] is best explained with reference to the elision of a preparation or of the consonant beginning of a passing-tone motion.

When, for example, Brahms, in the last movement of his Fourth Symphony, writes:

Example 150. Brahms, Fourth Symphony, Last Movement

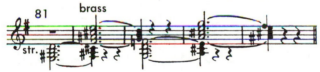

we find here that a seventh-chord is applied to each bass note (*E, F♯, G, A*); in each case we can assume an implicit preparation, or, in the last analysis, also a passing motion whose consonant initial interval has been elided.

With this doubt [about the independence of such apparently free dissonances] Schenker has moved beyond the "chordal" view of seventh chords. In his *Harmony* he still adhered to this view as well as to the theory of construction in thirds,

nance," *Journal of Music Theory* 6/2 (Winter 1962), p. 226ff.; also C. P. E. Bach, *Essay on the True Art of Playing Keyboard Instruments*, trans. and ed. by W. J. Mitchell (New York: Norton, 1949), p. 260, figure 335 and the accompanying discussion.]

[65. *Vierklänge*, literally "four-note chords," including specifically those designated 7, $\frac{6}{5}$, $\frac{4}{3}$, and $\frac{4}{2}$ in figured bass.]

and he characterized the V^7 as the sum of $V^5_3 + VII^5_3$.[66] Concerning the ultimate break with this point of view and the derivation of V^7 from voice leading:

Example 151.

see sections 4, 7, and 8.

In the fifth species of counterpoint we learn a kind of resolution of the syncope that provides a glimpse into the world of free composition. Specifically, it is possible in fifth species to lead the syncope before its resolution to a different tone, provided that this tone is consonant with the cantus-firmus tone:

Example 152.

From there it is but a short step to the substitute resolution of free composition, such as that in example 153.

Example 153.   Chopin, Prelude in Bb Major, op. 28 no. 21

The *ideal presence of the chord* that is here composed-out makes possible this leap [away from the dissonant tone]. Even the cantus-firmus tone presents itself similarly as an ideal entity, although in strict counterpoint the [explicit] tone of resolution remains a necessity.[67]

66. And yet even there we read on p. 188: "The fact that the seventh chord oversteps the boundary set by nature and thus is to be regarded purely as a *product of art. . . .*" [Translation modified. (Actually Schenker's explanation in *Harmony* of the seventh chord as an interlocking of two triads is not limited to the V^7: it applies to other seventh chords as well.)]

[67. This is a highly significant paragraph. Because the $^6_3$ sonority above Eb in example 153 is composed-out (in the left hand), its ideal presence in our imagination assumes a magnitude far greater than that which would result from an unelaborated presentation

And it is significant that Schenker writes, concerning the substitute resolution, in *Kontrapunkt I*, p. 435, "What an extremely fruitful principle! Its basis is, quite simply, that in free composition we are able to conceive all harmonies, under the guidance of the scale degrees, in an abstract and ideal manner—as though they rest on the foundation of the literal voice leading."

Apropos of substitution, which so clearly represents free composition as a prolongation of strict counterpoint, Schenker also speaks of leaping passing tones as a verification. In his discussion of the example from Handel's *G*-Major Chaconne (see example 154),[68]

Example 154. Handel, Chaconne in G Major, HHA IV/5,11, variation II

he shows how, by virtue of the governing *idea* of the chord, in essence even these passing tones approached by leap are to be traced back to the basic form of passing motion. And, in adumbration of the essential content of his theory of fundamental structure *(Ursatz)*, he writes,

> One sees, then, how one and the same basic phenomenon is manifested in so many forms, yet without completely losing its identity in any of them! However much a given variant may conceal the basic form, it is still the latter alone that occasions and fructifies the new manifestation. But to reveal the basic form together with its variants, and to uncover only *prolongations of a fundamental law* even where apparent contradictions hold sway—this is solely the task of counterpoint![69]

of the lower voices. It is this intensified presence of the sonority that enables the ear to accept as implicit a resolution of the suspended seventh: the composed-out chord establishes a gravitational field, as it were, into which the suspended seventh is ineluctably drawn. Even a cantus-firmus tone manifests this ideal quality to a limited extent, but not sufficiently to clarify and make convincing an implicit resolution along with a leap away from a suspended dissonance. Thus the necessity in strict counterpoint of the explicit tone of resolution is more than merely a procedural rule: it reflects the essential limitation of the resources at hand.]

[68. *Kontrapunkt I*, p. 314.]

69. *Kontrapunkt I*, p. 315.

Section 4.   The Occurrence of Dissonance in a Consonant State

The essential quality of dissonance is its passing character.[70] Movement and direction toward a specific goal are proper to it. The only sonority that can be composed-out is a stable one, thus a consonance. If composing-out is to be applied to a dissonance, it must temporarily be divested of its character of driving toward a goal; that is, the dissonant tone must be transformed into a consonance. (See the remarks to example 88a above.)

We encountered such cases already in connection with the third-progression and the mutually supportive character of two dissonant passing tones progressing in parallel motion. [See example 89.] And [we saw similar cases] in relation to the upper-fifth divider, which, as a leaping passing tone, made the dissonant passing tone of the upper voice consonant. (See example 91 [and chapter 2, section 2].) But if we set above this divider a motion from the fifth to the third, instead of from the third to the root:

Example 155.

then we see that the divider coincides with the passing tone in a dissonant interval, the seventh. This divider model shows us the birthplace of the so-called dominant-seventh chord. (See section 7.) Of special interest for our considerations is the dissonant condition of the passing tone, which is actually emphasized by the divider. In this case, then, more specialized procedures are required to make the passing tone consonant. In view of the extraordinary significance of the passing seventh over V, this case is particularly important. Because of the necessity to precede the seventh with a consonant interval (see example 156),

Example 156.

this procedure comes close to the [dissonant] syncope with its consonant preparation.[71] The appearance of the passing seventh in a consonant state in most cases forms the content of the middle section of three-part pieces whose

---

70. "The dissonance is always passing, never a chord member." Schenker, *Jahrbuch II*, p. 24.

71. To this category belong also, as similar cases, examples 129 and 130.

first section had moved to the dominant, above which the seventh, bringing about a *return* to the tonic, now passes:[72]

Example 157.   Bach, French Suite in E♭ Major, Sarabande

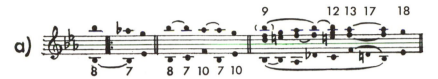

[72. The interpretative sketch is correct but potentially misleading. Although the ab^2 is given consonant support at bar 13—a support that is maintained through bar 16 by a descending third-progression in the upper voice—and returns as a dissonance at bar 17, the E♭ harmony that follows in bars 18–19 is not the definitive return of the tonic, nor does it provide the ultimate continuation of the passing ab. It is a stepping stone toward an A♭ sonority (not shown) that arrives in bar 20. The latter counts merely as the third of the *F*-minor sound of bars 13–16. The true V arrives in bar 21 and is prolonged through bar 22, where ab^2 returns. At a level deeper than that depicted in the sketch at b), it is *this* ab^2 that becomes the dissonant seventh and moves on to g^2 above the true I at the beginning of bar 23. The voice leading of the larger context is shown in appendix C, Supplementary Examples.]

The chord in which the tone representing the seventh appears as a consonance can be realized as an independent triad; it can even be tonicized and be subjected to its own composing-out. The seventh-tone usually occurs as a third or octave, less often as a fifth. Schematically, the possibilities are:

Example 158.

[Before we move on,] one more simple example [may be given] in which, within V, the seventh is temporarily made consonant by a simple passing tone in the lower voice, as in examples 129 and 130:

Example 159.   Beethoven, Bagatelle in G Major, op. 126 no. 1

The passing c^2 here is taken over from the middle voice [c^1 of bar 2].

Brahms's Intermezzo op. 76 no. 4 gains a special charm by virtue of the iridescent character that the passing seventh eb (within V of Bb) and its descent to d obtain as a result of the neighboring-tone and passing-tone motions of the bass. This is a piece whose content grows out of an extraordinary expansion of V.

Now, examples of sevenths whose purpose is to lead back to the tonic [after a tonicization of V].[73]

Example 160.   Mozart, Rondo in D Major, K. 485

If the seventh is introduced as an octave, the motion of the bass to the subdominant can be prolonged.

In the following example, the seventh appears as a third within a chord that can be regarded as a II (as in example 157):

[73. Additional interpretation is provided in appendix C, Supplementary Examples.]

Example 161. Beethoven, Sonata in G Major, op. 49 no. 2

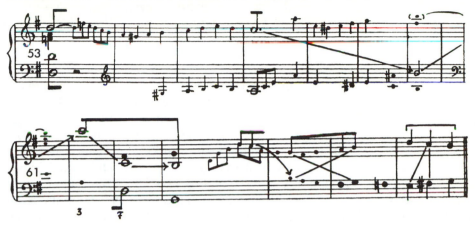

Section 5. Registral Manipulation of Voices

a. The Exchange of Voices

Exchange of voices serves the needs of composing-out and expansion of a chord. It brings about the transferral of a chordal tone from one voice into another; the tone that is transferred simultaneously trades places with another tone of the same chord. We have already encountered a particular type of exchange of voices, *voice crossing*, from the alignment in contrary motion of two third-progressions (see example 125). Voice crossing promotes the delineation *(Gestaltung)* of a chord as a unified whole. In the following example, it is assigned a prominent role with respect to synthesis and inner coherence:

Example 162. Mozart, Sonata in A Minor, K. 310, Development

At bar 70, the upper voice has moved from g^2 at the beginning of the development to f^2. At the same time, the bass has climbed from c to the passing tone
d; the two voices are now to converge on the octave e. At this point a motivic
problem arises for the forthcoming recapitulation. The first theme of the sonata
began with an appoggiatura $d\sharp^2$. But the upper voice, on the basis of the voice
leading indicated above, comes directly from f^2, and the lower voice from d.
This could have resulted in a purely mechanical quotation of the appoggiatura.
Mozart solves this problem by composing-out a voice crossing that transfers d
of the bass into the upper voice as $d\sharp^2$ while f^2 of the upper voice is taken
over by the bass; the appoggiatura tone d$\sharp$ is thus introduced *organically*, so
that a quotation of the appoggiatura itself is made unnecessary. This voice crossing
could have been carried out by simple third-progressions; but Mozart expands
the third-progression of the bass by inverting it to a sixth (see the beam beginning
in bar 70), follows with the upper voice in parallel tenths, averts potential parallel
fifths by means of interpolated sixths in the weak halves of the respective measures
(see the next section), and moreover accelerates the tempo of the linear progression
in the fourth bar.[74]

Even on a small scale—as though in a nutshell—voice crossings can produce
marvelous effects. What a truly programmatic effect in the sixth line of the chorale
cited earlier (example 131), where Bach writes:

Example 163.   Bach, "Christus, der uns selig macht,"
Riemenschneider no. 81

und fälschlich ver - kla   -   get,

The cross-relation, therefore a "false" voice crossing—how profoundly it expresses
the meaning of the poetic line, and yet in a purely musical fashion. How thoroughly
this one bar overshadows a multitude of "expressive" lieder! (Observe too the
passing $^6_4$ chord on d brought about by the voice crossing.)

Obviously, a leaping passing tone can appear in one of the voices in place of
a linear progression:

Example 164.

---

74. At the decisive point in the voice leading, where the bass reaches the d, the motivic
events of the foreground also change!

A special form of voice-exchange that is often encountered consists in placing a tone of the lower voice into another voice by interval inversion, so that, for example, a third becomes a sixth. In fourth-progressions this voice-exchange usually takes on the character of an imitation [75] Motivic extensions can also be obtained from this voice-exchange.

Example 165. Mozart, String Quintet in C Minor, K. 406, First Movement, bar 66ff.

Exchange of voices is an important technique for extension of a sonority, since only the position of the chord is changed.

b. Ascending and Descending Register Transfer

We have already observed, in connection with the octave- and the seventh-progression, the possibility of expanding a voice by transferring it into a different octave position. Such a variation of register is also attainable by other means.

[75. For example, in example 165, the bass of the third bar imitates the soprano of the second, and vice versa.]

1.   Change of Register through Arpeggiation

A simple arpeggiation may appear in place of a linear progression:[76]

Example 166.   Bach, Partita in B♭ Major, Allemande

In the upper voice, c^2 [of the second bar] does not move to bb^1 but is carried over the arpeggiation f^2–ab^2 to c^3, which then continues to bb^2. [Compare example 56.] Octave coupling combined with change of register was discussed earlier, in connection with example 120.

2.   Change of Register through Reaching-Over

This technique consists in two succcessive inversions of an interval, so that the same interval reappears in a different register.[77]

---

76. In his citation of this example in *Harmony*—as part of his explanation of mixture—Schenker already hints at a unified interpretation of the arpeggiation by his reading of the harmony from the middle of the second to the beginning of the fourth bar as "F-major/minor: I ____." It is true that he also supplies the individual chords in quarter-note values with scale-degree interpretations, but these are written in parentheses and between the staves.

[77. The account of reaching-over given here does not completely represent Schenker's later definition of the concept. Briefly stated, reaching-over involves motion upward (either by step or by leap) that is carried out with aid of one or more descending stepwise motions. There are many ways in which the descending stepwise entrances can fit into the resulting overall ascending motion. In example 168, the stepwise entrances are f^2–eb^2 (bars 1–3), ab^2–g^2 (bars 4–5), and eb^3–db^3 in bar 6. (The first and last of these are not shown in the

Example 167.

The reaching-over technique is of great importance. Unless it is understood, the apparent leaps of a voice into other interval-tones (which represent nothing but superimposed inner voices) cannot be explained.

Example 168. Schubert, Waltz op. 9 no. 1

To understand sequential applications of reaching-over, it is helpful to imagine the normal progression that the variant stands for. In Brahms's Capriccio in *F♯* Minor, op. 76 no. 1, for example:

Example 169. Brahms, Capriccio in F♯ Minor, op. 76 no. 1

illustration that accompanies example 168.) Reaching-over can yield either an ascending linear progression, an ascending arpeggiation, or an ascending register transfer (as eb^2–db^3 in example 168). It is therefore a general technique that serves any of several purposes. See *Free Composition*, pp. 47–49 and fig. 41.]

the voice leading stands for:

Example 170.

4-prg.

This voice-leading progression orients us with respect to the interpolations brought about by the ascending register transfer. (Compare also example 190.)

The external appearance of a repetition can be completely altered when it is combined with a change of register. This is the case in Beethoven's Sonata op. 110, bar 5ff. (see example 6): the third of bar 1, c^2-ab^1, is inverted at bar 5 into a rising sixth; the inner voice thus becomes the upper voice, as bar 6 clearly shows. Bar 9 presents ab^2 again as inner voice, and eb^2 of the preceding bar emerges an octave higher as the upper voice, so that bar 10 once again represents the situation of bar 3 transposed up an octave, which is expressed also by the motivic association. The ascending register transfer is combined with an enlargement: bar 5 stands for bar 1, bars 6 and 7 for bar 2, and bars 8–10 for bar 3. The motion of the bass underscores this in the clearest way; in addition, bar 9 contains a tonicization of the Db chord that follows:

Example 171. Beethoven, Sonata in Ab Major, op. 110, bar 5ff.

The following passage from Mozart's Bb Sonata, K. 333, quoted by Schenker in *Harmony* with reference to mixture, shows a descending register transfer in which bb^2 moves to a^1:

Example 172. Mozart, Sonata in B♭ Major, K. 333, First Movement, bar 59ff.

Through registral manipulations of this kind a sonority can be given a broader expansion:

Example 173. Beethoven, Sonata in E Minor, op. 90, bar 99ff.

In the second bar, f^1 is transferred to the higher octave, from which it falls chromatically to g^1; thence to the neighboring-tone ab, whereby the ascending second is transformed into a descending seventh. This ab is also reached by a chromatic descent—but now without chords (note the *cresc.*)—and at the same time the bass begins its passing motion through the octave. The neighboring tone *ab* goes first to *g*, which however is immediately restored to the higher register as g^1.[78]

Example 174.

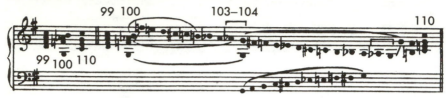

Section 6.   Octaves and Fifths

Strict counterpoint disallows the approach to perfect consonances by similar motion. It permits such approach neither from a perfect consonance of the same size (parallel motion) nor from a different perfect consonance or an imperfect consonance ("hidden" parallels). The reason for this prohibition in the case of the octave is easy to understand. Since the octave really represents a repetition of the same tone in a different register, if two or more octaves occur in succession, the result is a reduction in the number of voices; for example, in a two-voice setting, one of the voices would temporarily disappear, and, along with it, the rationale of the intended two-voice setting. The octave acts merely as a doubling; if, in a particular instance, it is not intended to act as such,[79] this must be sufficiently emphasized by what precedes and follows it. But even the succession of two octaves brings the sense of doubling into the foreground. Of course, this must not be confused with an intentional doubling used to strengthen sonority, for which, however, strict counterpoint offers no motivation.

The problem of fifths is more difficult. It has often been claimed that the same principle applies here—namely, that the fifth projects so strongly as an overtone that it, too, acts as a mere doubling. But certain facts argue against this explanation. First, there is the undeniable truth that the ear reacts differently, and indeed much more negatively, to a "fifth-doubling." And there is also a historical reason. The first attempts at polyphony sought, for reasons that were naive but therefore all the more understandable, to produce polyphony with the aid of the perfect consonances. This so-called *organum* actually represented a form of accompanimental doubling in perfect intervals. But as soon as thirds and sixths began to

---

78. In *Harmony*, p. 200, Schenker writes as follows about this passage: "The domination of the fifth scale-step, conceived as a unifying regulator, is so strong that all individual phenomena, among which are several diminished-seventh chords, assume the character of mere passing notes." How clearly the notion of prolongation of a scale step is conceived even here, albeit without a description of the voice leading of the particular case.

[79. That is, if the obligato character of the added voice is to be preserved in spite of the octave.]

be intermixed, the deficiency of the fifth was immediately revealed. The reason therefore must lie in the nature of the fifth itself.

The fifth is the boundary interval of the triad. It underscores most emphatically the root-potential of the lowest tone and therefore contributes significantly to its quality of immobility. When the ear, having extricated itself only with effort from an intervallic situation of this kind, is immediately placed in an identical situation in relation to another tone, it is unable to find adequate orientation with respect to the intended tonal environment. The ear becomes irritated and tries in vain to find a relationship between the two fifths that have simply been juxtaposed. As a consequence of its stationary quality, the fifth applies a brake that arrests motion. The characteristic element of motion is the sixth, because it does not rest at peace in itself, but, in a sense, always moves on in search of the root. Thus the sixth—and in counterpoint of three or more voices, the $\frac{6}{3}$ chord— becomes the soul of voice leading.[80]

It is not possible to deal here with all of the ways [parallel] fifths and octaves can be avoided, nor with the historical development of these possibilities and the variants offered by increasing numbers of voices and by the different species. The most important methods are these: successive fifths are averted through interpolated sixths, octaves through interpolated tenths:

Example 175.

5   6   5   8   10   8

In counterpoint of more than two voices, the poor effect of non-parallel similar motion to a perfect consonance can be reduced or even eliminated by the prominence of contrary motion in other voices. Therefore we shall deal here only with

---

[80. The explanations given here of the voice-leading constraints on perfect fifths and octaves apply only to parallel motion, not to non-parallel similar motion (so-called "hidden" octaves and fifths). These explanations may be supplemented with those given by Schenker in *Kontrapunkt I*, p. 176ff. Schenker derives the prohibition of similar motion to perfect consonances from the combination of two factors: (1) the intrinsic qualities of perfect intervals, and (2) the particular effect of similar motion. He observes, as Jonas does, that the octave is merely a duplication of the cantus tone, and that the fifth is the boundary interval of the triad; for these reasons, the perfect consonances tend to inhibit rather than promote contrapuntal fluidity. From this it follows that they do not make a good effect in contrapuntal settings if they are emphasized by appearing to be sought out for their own sake. But similar motion produces exactly this result: the voices appear to work in collaboration rather than independently, and thus to strive toward the perfect interval as a goal in itself. If a perfect interval comes about by contrary (or oblique) motion, on the other hand, its occurrence can be "written off" as a by-product of the independent motions of the voices. *Parallel* motion, incidentally, would thus be automatically excluded as a special (and particularly noxious) case of similar motion.]

parallel progressions.[81] The decisive factors always are first the setting of the outer voices, and then the relationship of upper and inner voices to the lowest voice. What is the situation in free composition with respect to all this? There is no issue that exposes the general misunderstanding of strict counterpoint and free composition [and their relation to each other] so blatantly as that of the prohibition of parallel successions. These parallel motions are the familiar "errors" that pedants point to when they would reject a composition as a whole; on the other hand, they are also those errors[82] that "progressives" dismiss with sweeping gestures and assure us that, after all, both the ancients and the greatest masters wrote "fifths." What is the truth of the matter? Whoever understands Schenker's theory of prolongation can solve this riddle easily. What was said above, at the beginning of this chapter in reference to example 79, applies here as well. The common error has been to apply the phenomena of strict counterpoint, which represent underlying patterns, *directly* to the work of art, without comprehending the forms of prolongation. For a complete understanding, it is necessary to penetrate to the background; those who are able to do so will discover there a scrupulous avoidance of all parallel motion in perfect intervals.[83] They will also see how precisely the necessity of this avoidance usually provides a source for the most beautiful configurations of voice leading and prolongation, and how the prohibition (in a higher, more profound sense—not simply as a "rule") has served as an immense fount of inspiration for our masters. Where parallels occur in the foreground of masterworks, in most cases they will find their justification in the voice leading of the background. In such cases, therefore, they simply don't really exist. All that is necessary is to understand the composing-out, which causes intervals to appear in the foreground that are different from the intervals of the background. (See example 79.) Johannes Brahms collected, on a series of pages now in the possession of the Gesellschaft der Musikfreunde, Vienna, examples of octaves and fifths from the broadest variety of works.[84] Through his remarks on these pages we find Brahms arriving at the following important insights: "One sees, and especially one hears, that no *progression* of two fifths occurs."[85] Further: "NB: Where do the truly *bad* fifths and octaves remain, and where

------

[81. The issue to be addressed, specifically, is how underlying parallel motions can be counteracted by voice-leading strata closer to the surface, and, in the opposite direction, superficial parallelisms are often justified and explained by deeper strata.]

[82. Here without quotation marks: in the context of this clause—that is, as they are committed by the "progressives" *(Fortschrittler)* referred to—they are truly *errors*, flaws in composing.]

[83. "Background" is used in a general sense here to mean "strata beneath the surface." See Schenker, *Free Composition*, pp. 57–60.]

84. Schenker published a facsimile edition of these pages, with explanatory commentary [(Vienna: Universal Edition, 1933). See Paul Mast, "Brahms's Study, Octaven u. Quinten u. A., with Schenker's Commentary Translated," *Music Forum V* (1980). Mast provides transcriptions as well as facsimiles of the manuscript pages, and an appendix with additional explanatory commentary on the examples.]

[85. MS p. 5; see Mast, pp. 84–85.]

can they be found[?]"[86] And finally: "Aside from mere carelessness or oversight, when and where one finds consecutive fifths that are actually bad, usually everything else is equally bad, so that the one fault is beyond consideration."[87] Here it is clearly voiced. The physiognomy of the total voice leading must be taken into consideration and must be judged before one can reach a decision regarding successive fifths and octaves. First an example of such "foreground fifths" from Brahms's notebook, p. 1, system 2 (Schumann, *Romanze* op. 28 no. 1):[88]

Example 176.   Schumann, *Romanze* op. 28 no. 1

At b) Schenker's explanation is given. The passing *F♯* of the bass appears as an accented passing tone; the resulting fifth is a coincidental collision of tones that has no place in the essential voice leading.

An example from a work by Brahms himself (the Sextet in *B♭*, op. 18, last movement):

Example 177.   Brahms, Sextet in B♭ Major, op. 18, Last Movement

The illustration at b again shows how the first bar really should be heard. The justaposition of fifths is coincidental.[89]

[86. MS p. 8; see Mast, pp. 112–113.]

[87. MS p. 2; see Mast, pp. 42–43.]

[88. See Mast, pp. 28–29.]

89. Those who are unable to hear organically and follow the sense of composing-out will hear parallel fifths in these cases. Kurth writes (in *Grundlagen des linearen Kontrapunkts* [p. 477]): "A series of directly successive, *open* parallel fifths is also found, for example, in the contrapuntally highly interesting Duet for Clavier in *E* Minor [BWV 802]

We turn now to procedures for avoiding the real parallels. When the outer voices move in tenths, the danger of parallel fifths between bass and inner voice arises. See example 120, and the tenths indicated there. Example 179 again presents the succession of fifths to be avoided [together with the voice leading used to avoid them]:[90]

Example 179.

When fifths ascend by step, a sixth is prefixed:

Example 180.   Brahms, Fourth Symphony, Last Movement

Chromatic motion in the lower voice is often combined with this procedure; this results in tonicization. The root of the inserted sixth chord can be added in

---

by Bach . . . . The fifths . . . are possible only because the tones are immediately continued chromatically (in both voices, in the present case):"

Example 178.   Bach, Duet for Clavier in E Minor, BWV 802

This way of hearing, which completely fails to recognize the suspension character of the *a♯* and the *g♯* and the [essential] sixths [that follow them], forms the basis of a whole book on Bach!

90. Compare also example 116.

the bass; the chord is thus expanded into a sonority capable of being composed-out:[91]

Example 181.   Beethoven, Sonata in E♭ Major, op. 81a, Last Movement

The next expansion can involve leading the lowest voice upward through a sixth-progression, thus to the sixth that [in the background] belongs to the inner voice:

Example 182.   Scarlatti, Sonata in B♭ Major, K. 551

a)

b)

---

91. See example 88a. [Also fn. 92 below, and the illustration.]

Thus there arise apparently independent, "harmonic" sonorities that really derive their cause and logic entirely from voice leading. The root-defining quality of the fifth here celebrates its highest triumph, in that it is preceded by a chord that sounds like a dominant in relation to it. Such tonicizing chords, which originate in the sixths interpolated for the purpose of avoiding parallel fifths, will always appear when the bass moves upward by step. The most common cases in larger contexts are those having to do with the cadence IV—V—I, where the juxtaposition of the fourth and fifth degrees harbors the danger of parallel fifths and necessitates an interpolation to avoid them. (See section 7, below.)

This necessity for a corrective in voice leading sheds light again on the artificial character of the fourth scale degree and the juxtaposition of IV and V. The preference here was to fashion, through voice leading, a relationship organized by fifths: II—V—I.[92] Related to the cadential progression IV—V—I is the movement, for example, from I through II to V, in which the V is tonicized and stabilized by means of II with a raised third.

Example 183.

$$E \quad I \quad (VI\sharp) \quad II\sharp \quad V$$
$$5 \ - \ 6 \ - \ 5$$

[92. The clearest case is where, in a cadential progression IV—V—I, a 5–6 replacement occurs over IV. Such a replacement originates purely in voice leading, but the $\frac{6}{3}$ chord above IV that is thus produced happens to be identical to a "first inversion" of II; therefore, as a by-product of voice leading, at least the illusion of a "harmonic" progression by fifths results. It should be emphasized that voice leading remains the principal determining factor, even where the bass, by moving chromatically as the sixth enters, produces the effect of an applied dominant to V: the sixth anticipates the fifth of the coming V and thus mediates between IV⁵ and V⁵. The first two bars of example 199 are interesting in this connection. Here there is no 5–6 replacement; rather, the *f* bass on the second quarter is set with a $\frac{6}{3}$ at its arrival. Yet there is no doubt that a significant function of the sixth above *f* (which produces a II⁶ of *C* major) is to anticipate the fifth of the following *g* and thus to suppress any possible impression of parallel fifths. This discussion of the 5–6 alternation as a technique for the suppression of parallel fifths is apposite to the remarks on p. 25 concerning the juxtaposition of IV and V, along with the first introduction of cadences, and also to the comments preceding and following example 36: the use of VI as the third upper fifth takes us into "the realm of actual voice leading" in the sense that VI, as a buffer between I and II, can also be understood as the result of adding *above* I a sixth that anticipates the fifth of II. Thus in the progression I—VI—II, even if the VI appears in "root position," at a deeper level the structure is I $\overset{5-6}{\underline{\quad\quad}}$ II, and it can therefore be traced back to the realm of actual voice leading. Again, this will apply equally

This motion in the foreground is generally referred to as modulation:[93]

Example 184. Beethoven, Sonata in E Major, op. 14 no. 1

Beethoven achieves a most intimate connection of the formal sections in the first movement of the Eighth Symphony, in which the second theme enters early, as shown below, without waiting for the arrival at the harmonic goal:

well where the tonic tone is raised chromatically at the arrival of VI to produce the effect of an applied dominant to II:

Brahms, Violin Sonata in A Major, op. 100

Once again, voice leading yields as a by-product a fifth-relationship—here, between VI♯ and II.]

93. Schenker rejects the concept of modulation. The notion of background, the unity of the work of art, and the concept of tonality as a unified whole cannot be reconciled with the assumption of true modulations. (See chap. 4.)

Example 185.   Beethoven, Eighth Symphony, First Movement

Here the sixth *f–d* is unfolded and composed-out. Expanded to a *D*-major chord, it is motivically fitted to the new thematic idea and stabilized by the A^7 chord that precedes it. Only those who understand the background origin, the underlying voice leading, and the growth from that voice leading of a colorful harmony that can be composed-out, will grasp the true coherence of this passage.[94] Without this relationship to the background, individual events become an arbitrary succession.

The collaboration of principles of voice leading (5–6–5) and harmony (V—I) cannot be overemphasized.

Here again is a proof against the theory of functional harmony, since the procedures described can of course involve all scale degrees of the system. The frequent occurrence of the succession IV—V in practice, however, has led to a peculiarity. Instead of simply *displacing* the fifth [of IV], the sixth that anticipates [the fifth of V] has often been *added* to it, as though special precautions were desirable because of the coming V. This produced the $\frac{6}{5}$ chord on degree IV, which has cost the theorists so much mental anguish, for all of which they still failed to recognize it as a manifestation of the 5–6 motion of counterpoint. (More about this in the next section.)

[94. "And how much Beethoven's performance indications contribute: they specify *p dolce* only at the repetition of the motive, when it appears in *C*, whereas the first time— still in *D* major—*sempre p!*" Jonas, "Beethoveniana," *Der Dreiklang 6* (September, 1937), pp. 156–157.]

Now, a few examples of the avoidance of octaves. A simple one, mentioned already in connection with the seventh-progression:

Example 186. Schubert, Waltz op. 9 no. 36

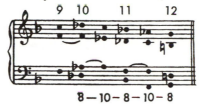

Next, a prolongation that is more difficult to hear:

Example 187. Brahms, Rhapsody in G Minor, op. 79 no. 2

Where the neighboring tone e^2 of the upper voice coincides with the passing-tone E of the bass, the threat of parallel octaves arises. Their avoidance through the interpolated tenth is prolonged, in that the motion is expanded into a sixth-progression (d–b) and, above the bass B, d of the top voice is led chromatically through $d\sharp$. Thus a B-major chord arises; it has a tonicizing effect on the following e-minor chord, which belongs to the passing motion. How well this expansion of V—I with its passing chords is suited to the rhapsodic character intended here!

Section 7.   The "Dominant-Seventh Chord" and the "$^6_5$ Chord on IV"

In the foregoing account it has been shown how all composing-out of the nature-based triadic concept came about through voice leading and how this concept attained artistic vitality by being set in motion. Arpeggiation and passing tone have been cited as the elements that generate art. Among other things, we became acquainted with the 5–6 displacement as the motor capable of pushing aside the static fifth. As mentioned above, the frequent juxtaposition of IV and V occasioned an abbreviation of the displacement procedure: there arose the formation IV$^6_5$, which had the appearance of an independent chord and which, because of its contradiction of nature, necessarily posed riddles for those who failed to understand its origin. It was like a word whose original meaning has gradually disappeared, and which is now used only as a token. Motion became paralyzed. A phenomenon that had derived its sense from the horizontal dimension turned into a pseudo-vertical entity. The fact that the procedure of the anticipating sixth was possible on all scale degrees—that the difference lay merely in the frequency of usage—was not able to forestall misunderstanding. The listener, incapable of grasping organic coherence, failed to pursue origin and goal and to seek out the true meaning; his laziness transformed the finely woven voice-leading fabric into a series of tone-lumps. From the fluid, deeply meaningful texture there arose the "$^6_5$ chord."

A similar fate befell the seventh of V. Having originated as passing tone—from motion, from melody—, the seventh had in addition a particular mission within the tonal system. Because the seventh deprived the tone above which it moved of its root-potential,[95] or, more accurately, placed itself in contradiction to that root-potential, it certified that tone as representative merely of a fifth scale-degree [instead of a tonic]. If a piece moved to the [fifth-] divider by way of arpeggiation—thus in a chordal-harmonic way—, this procedure found a welcome melodic response in the seventh.[96] This procedure suggested, however, that

---

[95. *Grundtonhaftigkeit*. The term is used here actually in a freer sense that would be more exactly represented by the expression "tonic-potential," which can be understood as a ramification of root-potential.]

[96. That is, the harmonic motion of the bass—the leap of a fifth from I to V—found an agreeable contrast in the melodic motion 8–7 that followed above the so-achieved dominant.]

any tone could be characterized as a V by merely "imposing" the seventh above it. This abbreviated process led to the misconception that the resulting structures represented finished chordal products, so to speak. Again a formation of voice leading was frozen into a vertical event. The misunderstanding was more conspicuous here than in the preceding example: theory spoke of the necessity for "resolution of the seventh chord" and failed to notice that this necessity resulted (and could only have resulted) from the fact that the seventh stood for a motion that had already been initiated and that now demanded continuation. The attempt was made to explain the seventh exclusively as a vertical phenomenon, and thus evolved the completely schematic conception of chord structure as organized in thirds. If the most serious offense against nature had been to regard the fifth as a conjunction of two thirds—the fifth, on the contrary, occurs in the overtone series before the third—, the explanation of the seventh-chord just described led to still worse consequences. Why should one stop at the stacking-up of three thirds and not continue further to "construct" still more new "chords"? At the same time, the invertibility of chords was taught, and also the reducibility of all sonorities to certain root-position chords—a lamentable situation and a tragic loss for art music. The whole of music became truly paralyzed in these few chords: from the terse 5–6 displacement there arose the $\frac{6}{5}$ chord, and from the passing motion $\frac{8\text{–}7\text{–}3}{\text{V}\text{—}\text{I}}$—a source of movement and life—the dominant-seventh chord.[97] This *chordal* interpretation [of originally melodic phenomena] harbored within itself the great danger that all passing and incidental events would now be certified as chords. It is nothing short of grotesque when Schoenberg, in his *Harmonielehre*, cites as a proof of the correctness of his piled-up chordal formations his contention that the seventh chord, indeed, occurred only in passing "before it was incorporated into the system."[98]

How thoroughly the seventh was and should be heard "melodically," therefore horizontally, is shown by a particular form of linkage technique used by our masters:

Example 188. Mozart, Sonata in F Major, K. 332

[97. It is not, of course, the mere evolution of these chords as vertical structures that is considered harmful, but their misunderstanding by musicians, and the further consequences of that misunderstanding.]

98. Schoenberg, *Harmonielehre*, [p. 390].

In bar 4 there is as yet no definitive sense of closure; this is connected with the fact that bb^1 is placed by a voice-exchange[99] into a lower register in which it is then led onward. In the melodic domain, however, the ear remains altogether unsatisfied; it desires an appropriate continuation in the register of the upper voice. Thus in spite of the harmonic closure the need for continuation persists. How marvelously Mozart repeats in summation (in the following upbeat, before the a arrives in the next bar) the preceding motion [from c to bb, in bars 10–11 of the example].[100]

Section 8.   Critique of Previous Theories

Rameau's *Traité de l'harmonie*[101] appeared in 1722. It presented the theory of the invertibility of chords and the attendant concept of the fundamental bass. Although the observation that a harmony remains the same regardless of the registral position of its components was instructive for the concept of scale-degree, the formulation of it offered by Rameau was in equal measure obfuscating and disastrous. Rameau was not on the same level as his great contemporaries; he had no ear for the inner connections in their works, and, above all, had no notion that voice leading serves the composing-out of larger harmonic regions. He identified chord with scale degree, reduced every simultaneity to so-called root position, and rent the artistic fabric of voice leading into tatters of chords strung together without relationship.[102] The chord, which had acquired its logic and meaning from its context, now stood only for itself, without necessary relationship to what preceded or followed. The bass voice, which no less than the other voices represented a meaningful composing-out of a sonority, was burdened tone by tone with the

---

[99. This term is again used freely here; it means merely that an inner voice takes over the bb, rather than that two voices literally exchange tones.]

100. The masters also like to introduce the seventh as a passing tone even when it could simply be carried over (as a syncope) from before; they do this by moving first to an upper neighbor, from which the seventh then enters as a passing tone. See example 144b, where c^2 first moves to d^2.

[101. Translated, with an introduction and notes, by Philip Gossett as *Treatise on Harmony* (New York: Dover Publications, 1971).]

[102. In the introduction by Jonas to Schenker's *Harmony*, parts of this section appear in a kind of paraphrased translation; there, instead of chords strung together "without relationship," Jonas speaks of "more or less closely related chords." It is true that Rameau, in his efforts to formulate laws governing the progression of his fundamental bass, did concern himself to a limited extent with the horizontal dimension; but he gave little if any attention to relationships other than those between pairs of adjacent chords.]

leaden weights of the fundamental bass, which inhibited motion. All the tonal life congealed. In the same year 1722, when Bach produced the first volume of his *Well-Tempered Clavier* with its miracles of voice leading, from another quarter the seeds of destruction for music were sown.

To state it first of all very concisely, Rameau's great error was to interpret harmonically, or vertically, a bass that was conceived horizontally, according to contrapuntal principles, from an ideal sonority. The process of composing-out was totally overlooked. With this kind of analysis, theory reflected the state of practice around 1500. As composers progressed from the beginnings of polyphony to the discovery of the vertical sonority, they began to depart from the paths of pure voice leading and began to think chordally, but merely from chord to chord, so to speak—that is, they set chord alongside chord in *root position*. Only later, when this chord-by-chord plodding had shown itself to be unfruitful and the reaction of monody had set in, did they learn to compose out a single sonority in the horizontal direction. The *thoroughbass*, which developed shortly thereafter, represents a composed-out bass voice, a successful attempt at horizontal unfolding. The upper voices, whose movement was directed by the continuo numerals, followed similar horizontal lines. To reduce this living bass line to a so-called fundamental bass was the most serious error of the new theory [of Rameau].

The penetration of this theory into practice precipitated the most frightful regression in musical evolution. The reception accorded this theory in Germany should have sufficed to discredit it thoroughly. Bach and his circle disapproved of it completely. C.P.E. Bach wrote to Kirnberger, a loyal student of Bach, regarding the controversy between Kirnberger and Marpurg: "You may announce it publicly that my father's principles and my own are anti-Rameau." Kirnberger himself wrote:

> Rameau has filled this theory with so many absurdities that it is simply amazing how such extravagances have been able to find believers, even defenders, among us Germans, since we have always had the greatest composers among us whose treatment of harmony was certainly not to be explained according to Rameau's doctrines. Some went so far that they preferred to deny the thoroughness of [even] Bach's procedure with respect to the treatment and progression of chords, rather than admit that the Frenchman could have been wrong.[103]

And in his *Reiner Satz*[104] (Vol. I, p. 248), Kirnberger writes:

> Rameau himself has not grasped the simplicity of harmony in its true purity; for he occasionally mistakes passing notes for fundamental ones. This is the

---

[103. Johann Philipp Kirnberger, *The True Principles for the Practice of Harmony*, trans. by David Beach and Jürgen Thym, in *Journal of Music Theory* 23/2 (Fall, 1979), p. 168. Originally *Die wahren Grundsätze zum Gebrauch der Harmonie* (Berlin and Königsberg, 1773).]

[104. Kirnberger, *Die Kunst des reinen Satzes in der Musik* (Berlin, 1771–79). Translated, by David Beach and Jürgen Thym, as *The Art of Strict Musical Composition* (New Haven: Yale University Press, forthcoming).]

basis of his "chord of the added sixth" [precisely the "$^6_5$ chord"], for example, which he regards as a fundamental chord.

In Germany at that time strict counterpoint was taught, according to the work of Johann Joseph Fux,[105] and, above all, the practical school of thoroughbass, which also represents a voice-leading theory. Because composers indicated the motion of the accompanying voices [of the continuo] only by figures and left the realization of these voices up to the performer, an understanding of and training in thoroughbass was an indispensable prerequisite for all who desired to cultivate music. The principal treatise was C.P.E. Bach's *Versuch über die wahre Art, das Clavier zu spielen* (Berlin, 1753 and 1762).[106] It was this work, and not, for example, the treatises of Rameau, that our masters studied. Haydn declared that C.P.E. Bach was the man to whom he owed everything; the *Versuch* was the textbook from which Haydn fashioned his expertise, and, along with Fux's work, the source from which he himself taught. Mozart studied the Bach treatise; Neefe gave it, along with Kirnberger's writings, to his pupil Beethoven. The masters studied *voice-leading theory*—pure counterpoint and practical thoroughbass; the [conventional] *harmony treatise*, which for decades has formed the principal subject matter of instruction, simply did not exist. It was a misfortune that as the thoroughbass fell into disuse in practice, its theoretical teaching also disappeared from instruction. Its voice-leading theory was corrupted by Rameau's fundamental-bass theory, and thus arose the harmony treatise, that strange conglomeration which unites voice leading and scale-degree theory in such an unsatisfactory way. For a while the old tradition endured; Mendelssohn certainly received instruction in the old manner from his teacher Zelter. (The efforts of C.P.E. Bach and Quantz in Berlin had not been in vain.) Could this have been the reason that Mendelssohn was the last who was capable of improvisation, an art greatly fostered by thoroughbass practice? Even Brahms was forced to complain about all that he "first had to unlearn" before he found the correct orientation.

Rameau's theory came to Germany through Kirnberger's antipode Marpurg, who translated d'Alembert's work on Rameau into German.[107] The theory was later transmitted also by Vogler, whose charlatanism is adequately documented in Mozart's letters.[108] Anyone not convinced by this need only glance at Vogler's

---

[105. Fux, *Gradus ad parnassum* (Vienna, 1725). The section on species counterpoint is translated and edited by Alfred Mann in Fux, *The Study of Counterpoint* (New York: Norton, 1943; 2nd ed. 1965). The discussion of fugal technique appears in English translation in Mann, *The Study of Fugue* (London: Faber and Faber, 1958).]

[106. Translated, by William J. Mitchell, as *Essay on the True Art of Playing Keyboard Instruments* (New York: Norton, 1949).]

[107. Jean le Rond d'Alembert, *Systematische Einleitung in die musikalische Setzkunst, nach den Lehrsätzen des Herrn Rameau* (Leipzig: Breitkopf, 1757).]

[108. Specifically, in letters written to his father from Mannheim on 8 November, 1777, 13 November, 1777, 20 November, 1777, and 17 January, 1778, among others. See Ludwig Schiedermair. *Die Briefe W. A. Mozarts und seiner Familie* (4 vols., Munich and Leipzig, 1914), vol. I, nos. 87, 90, 93, and 107.]

"Improvements of the Bach Chorales."[109] Unfortunately that childishly impudent piece of busy-work elicited admiration even from Vogler's pupil [Carl Maria von] Weber. Perhaps one can understand from this why Weber was not equal to the synthesis of the great masters. Or, we can observe the fruits of the Rameau theory in France itself; Berlioz, for example, whose most obvious failings, quite tellingly, are faulty construction of the bass (i.e., basses that lack composing-out) and the writing of empty chords without any vitalization through composing-out.[110] Composers learned to think in "chords"; they saw nothing but chords in the works of the masters, and, as a result, they themselves wrote nothing but chords. It should never have come to pass that the thoroughbass, after it had lost its practical utility, ceased also to be taught as theory. (Incidentally, thorough-bass continued to be even a practical necessity for the performance of old music.) Still less should the signatures of thoroughbass, which were a pure voice-leading language, have been reduced to a mere "chordal language" in the conventional harmony treatise. The thoroughbass figures specified the movement and progression of voices, not a static chordal structure. In Bach's chorales with figured bass we find the following:[111]

Example 189.

Isn't it clear from the indication 8–7 that Bach brings the seventh as a passing tone from the octave? Why [else] does he expressly write the 8, which would otherwise be superfluous? The figures show movement, not some kind of "seventh chord." In the second part of the example, where the figures express a slow turn—how could this be interpreted "chordally"?

And how would our understanding of the coherence of the following example benefit from a chordal interpretation with reduction to fundamental chords, as the conventional harmony treatise teaches?

[109. See Georg Joseph Vogler, *Betrachtungen der Mannheimer Tonschule* (3 vols; Mannheim, 1778–81), III.]

110. Schumann, who wanted to welcome everything new with an open mind and heart, writes in his review of the "Waverly" Overture [*Neue Zeitschrift für Musik* 10 (1839)], "Often it is only a series of empty sound effects, of lumps of chords thrown together, that seems to determine the character of the piece. . . ." Isn't the future course of development (as well as the current situation) foretold in this remark?—a course of development in which the figure of Brahms protrudes, larger than life, like a legacy of a bygone era.

[111. First example: "Auf, Auf! mein Herz mit Freuden," BWV 441; second example: "Lasset uns mit Jesu ziehen," BWV 481.]

Example 190. Beethoven, Sonata in C Major, op. 53, Second Movement

If we experiment with such an interpretation, the abstruse result is astonishing:

Example 191.

The truth is, rather, that the chords derive their meaning from the domain of voice leading. In the harmonic-chordal sense, there is [only] the *F*-major chord, manifested in the fundamental and its impulse toward the fifth. Thus the bass moves through a *fourth-progression*, from *F* to *C*. At the same time the *F* chord moves to a *C* chord as divider. (Observe the registral position, corresponding to the natural chord of the overtone series, of the *F* chord at the beginning.) The third, *a (tenuto!)*, moves to the fifth of the *C* chord *(sf!)*, while *c* moves to *bb* as a passing tone. This is accomplished through ascending register transfer with the aid of reaching-over, combined with chromaticism:

Example 192.

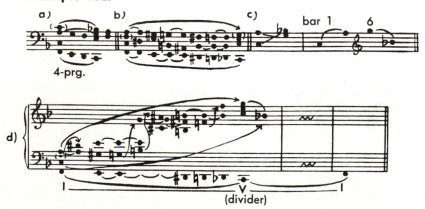

Here is truly meaningful coherence. The other interpretation is merely a useless spelling-exercise. To construe this passage in terms of chords and fundamental-bass notes amounts to the negation of voice leading and the distortion of content to the point of unrecognizability.

What can such a theory do when it encounters actual root-position chords (that is, chords that appear in root position in the foreground) such as the simple *C* chord that arises from the sixth inserted to avoid parallel fifths in example 181? Or, still worse, the more complex *C* chord that stems from the sixth *e–c* in example 88? This kind of theory not only neglects to trace such root-position chords back to the passing tones from which they originate and derive their meaning and connection: it rips apart the passing motions of the foreground by turning them into meaninglessly juxtaposed "fundamental chords." Is it not clear that such a perspective inevitably led to the decline of music? And all because of the failure to grasp the notion of the chord as an *ideal entity*, temporally manifested in music through voice leading and its prolongations. It had not been understood that the bass itself served composing-out, and therefore represented an upper voice of a *single* ideal tone, not of a "fundamental bass" that accompanied laboriously, weighting down each of its tones. The theory of the fundamental bass meant nothing less than the obliteration of contrapuntal thinking for the sake of so-called harmonic thinking, which rested on false premises. By reducing the passing sonority to a fundamental chord, this theory stripped that sonority of the logic and *significance* that it possessed as a passing event. The [Riemannian] theory of functional harmony, which had grown out of the need for a scale of valuation for sonorities, provided no aid by its reduction of all chords to tonic, dominant, or subdominant. This attempt had to fail, because it neglected the fact that two occurrences of the same chord could be worlds apart in meaning, and that everything depended on context.[112] Even the concept of "secondary dominant" *(Zwischendominante)* was only a makeshift, since it concerned only the relationship of two adjacent chords. And how could anyone hope to master large-scale synthesis [in this way]! Composers had learned only to listen laboriously from chord to chord in the works of the masters, and therefore they eventually lost the capacity for larger-scale conception. It was no wonder, then, that they took refuge in program and drama.

Just as a curiosity, and to show how such harmonic hearing and interpretation can even surpass a manner of composing—although the two are obviously interdependent—, an example from *Regers Harmonik* by H. Grabner[113] may be cited:

[112. The "functional" theory did recognize the influence of context in a very limited way. For example, III in a major key could be represented in such analyses either as the "relative" of the dominant or as the "leading-tone shift" of the tonic, depending upon context. But the theory fell far short of a recognition of the phenomenon of composing-out, and, as a result, failed to discriminate between vertically and horizontally generated chords.]

113. Hermann Grabner, *Regers Harmonik* [Munich: Halbreiter, 1920, p. 34.]

Example 193.   Reger, String Quartet op. 109 (after H. Grabner, *Regers Harmonik*)

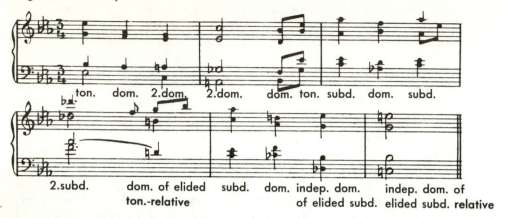

Need anything further be added?

The unrestrained overburdening of the vertical had to evoke a reaction. But the pendulum had swung too far in one direction for the countermotion to stop in the proper place. The theory of "linear counterpoint" arose, and with it the "linear" way of composing. This amounted to throwing the baby out with the bathwater. One thought and wrote horizontally, but without attending to the requirements given by nature in the triad, whose unfolding must be served by every horizontal succession and vertical combination. Only when the horizontal dimension serves the unfolding of a triad can the vertical relationships fall correctly into place. "Any closed melodic line weakens the vertical chords [that accompany it] with respect to their meanings as individuals in the same measure that the melodic line itself effects the composing out of a particular chord in the horizontal direction."[114] It is the essential part of Schenker's work, and his very great contribution, to have recognized and described the true relation between the horizontal and the vertical. How to satisfy the demands of harmony, to understand correctly the function of voice leading: this is what his theory shows us—a theory created from a profound knowledge of the masterworks and apperceived by listening with a gifted, artistic and re-creating ear: his theory of the *fundamental structure*.

---

114. Schenker, *Kontrapunkt II*, p. 18.

Chapter 4

The Theory of Fundamental Structure

If Nature in her lifeless beginnings had not been so thoroughly stereo-metric, how could she have finally produced such incalculable and immeasurable life?

Goethe

All religious experience, all philosophy and science strives toward the most concise formula. It was a similar impulse that led me to conceive of a musical composition as emanating from the core of a fundamental structure as the first composing-out of the basic triad (tonality). I *observed* the fundamental line *(Urlinie);* I did not deduce it.

Schenker, *Jahrbuch II*

Section 1. The Fundamental Line

It is absolutely necessary to ensure always that regardless of the rich variation, which is quite popular today, the basic lineaments of the piece, through which its affect is made known, show through clearly.

C. P. E. Bach

The goal of our presentation thus far has been to show how higher-level connections and unified wholes can be established in music. We have seen the triad as an ideal entity; its arpeggiation; its unfolding through the agency of voice leading. The linear progression as an entity reaching from its point of departure to its end point, and, moreover, deriving its unification from its ideally prolonged head-tone. The composing-out of a neighboring tone as an event that returns to its point of departure. Our presentation of Bach's *C*-Major Prelude (example 134) has already revealed how these entities fit together, how they combine to form a single larger entity that operates over the course of an entire piece, and how they are to be regarded as the unfolding and elaboration of precisely this larger entity. This final entity, the background, whose offshoots extend into the smallest details of the work of art, was revealed to Schenker in his theoretical concept of *fundamental structure*. To understand it properly, we must follow the path that led Schenker to this concept.

In section 2 of the first chapter we spoke of repetition as an artistic resource. Let us recall the passage quoted there from Mozart's *C*-Major Sonata (example 3). In spite of the difference, apparently so great, between bars 5ff. and what preceded, we discerned a relationship. Indeed, we identified a repetition. Now, consider Mozart's *C*-minor Fantasy, K. 396, bars 2–10:

Example 194.   Mozart, Fantasy in C Minor, K. 396, bar 2ff.

Observe the treatment of the stepwise descent from eb^2: an enlarged form in bars 7–10 and later in 11–16, and also the contraction to thirty-second notes of bars 9 and 10. It is clear that for these repetitions, which, more or less hidden, establish the coherence of a piece—literally representing its lifeblood and unifying substance—, Schenker could no longer find adequate the definition formulated in *Harmony* of motive as the repetition of a series of tones. Here we are dealing rather with repetitions that go beyond the motive, the explicit tonal analog of the word—repetitions that permeate and run through the course of an entire piece. Leaving aside Schenker's first attempts in the *Erläuterungsausgaben* of Beethoven's last five piano sonatas, and op. 101 in particular, Schenker first came to grips with the concept of the fundamental line in the first volume of *Der*

Tonwille (1921). The fundamental line marks Schenker's decisive effort to move from the phenomena of the foreground toward a background-oriented way of hearing. Through it, he penetrated to those forces that move so mysteriously in the works of genius and cause them to appear as though begotten by nature, invigorated by a *single* breath. The biological aspect, the life-impulse of tones, to which Schenker referred as early as *Harmony*, returns here. It is expressed in the title of his periodical *Der Tonwille (The Will of Tone)*. The formulation presented there may be quoted here in part:

> As suggested by the term itself, the fundamental line is a primal state *(Urzustand)*, a primordial succession of tones.
>
> The fundamental line holds in itself the seeds of all forces that generate tonal life: it is the fundamental line that, together with scale degrees, shows the correct path for all composing out and therefore also for the counterpoint of the outer voices, in whose intervals the union of strict counterpoint and free composition is consummated in such a marvelously mysterious way. It is the fundamental line, too, that gives life to motive and to melody. Only those who grasp the nature of the fundamental line will find access to its offspring, melody, and will understand that melody, because of its origin in the fundamental line, is far more than it is generally taken to be.
>
> Even the fundamental line itself fulfills the law of procreation (that is, the law of repetition), and, with such a primordial impulse *(Urtrieb)*, it takes its place in nature, with its continual activity of growing and multiplying; it becomes a vital part of nature. While motives and melodies dart about before our ear in repetitions that are easily identifiable as such, the primal womb of the fundamental line gives birth to repetitions of a hidden, highest order. Those who make light of repetitions and their driving force in music reveal that they hear only in the foreground—that they have as yet heard nothing of the primal force of the fundamental line's background repetitions.[1]

And further:

> The marvel of creation on a large scale is accomplished in the fundamental line. It is the muse that inspires all improvisatory creation and all synthesis. It is both beginning and end of a work: it is the work's whole inspiration. Through the fundamental line, the composer becomes a prophet. He is drawn to it as to mother earth,[2] and, as though intoxicated by its guidance and direction, he imparts to his tones a graced destiny full of harmonious accord between their innate life and a being that is above them and behind them (as a "platonic idea" in music)—a destiny full of discipline, custom, and order, even where the foreground appears to manifest rebellion, chaos, or dissolution.[3]

---

1. *Der Tonwille I* (1921), p. 22.
[2. *Wie zu den Ur-Müttern.*]
3. *Der Tonwille I* (1921), p. 23.

Part of the explanatory example from the same issue of *Der Tonwille* on Bach's Prelude in E♭ Minor, *Well-Tempered Clavier I,* may be cited here with Schenker's commentary:

Example 195.   Schenker, *Der Tonwille I,* p. 38

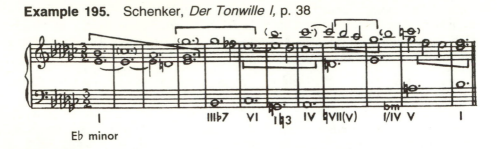

E♭ minor

Here we observe first of all that the fundamental line takes the form of a basically three-tone motive, whose urge toward self-propagation engenders countless repetitions. Such a motive, precisely because it encompasses three tones, is of itself merely a composing-out of one or another third-space; its repetition, too, is of itself nothing more than just a repetition; but here, how differently the motive is secured in each case, and how continually different are the repetitions![4]

This discussion shows clearly Schenker's direction. *Horizontal* hearing is once again to be given its rightful place: this means, hearing of the contrapuntal passing motions through all of the complexity of the foreground phenomena. The fundamental line is not a vague, arbitrary linear concept to Schenker, even at this early stage of his development; it is already "composing-out of a third-space," thus realization of a definite vertical concept in the horizontal plane.

Schenker's remark in *Harmony* (p. 306) on the following measure from Bach's *D*-minor Fugue, *Well-Tempered Clavier I,* is not without interest as a significant adumbration:

Example 196.   Bach, *WTC I,* Fugue in D Minor

The upper counterpoint . . . , for example, seems to grow out of the original or primary idea *(Uridee):*

---

4. "Joh. Seb. Bach: Wohltemperiertes Klavier, Band I. Praeludium Es-Moll," in *Der Tonwille I* (1921), p. 38.

Example 197. Schenker, *Harmony*, p. 306

passing through the intermediate stage of:[5]

Example 198. Schenker, *Harmony*, p. 306

Precisely because it represented a *first* attempt to hear horizontal paths in the work of art—to recognize basic contrapuntal formations such as passing tone, neighboring tone, etc., also in free composition—the hearing process at first was excessively bound to the upper voice. The fundamental line is after all a melodic concept, which is most at home in a higher register. Therefore it alone could not provide access to that precision necessary for an exhaustive understanding of the work of art. In the representation cited above of the E♭-minor Prelude, for example, the bass arpeggiation *eb-cb-ab* is still lacking; and thus, necessarily, a definitive clarification of the motion of the upper voice and its relation to this bass arpeggiation is also lacking. But this cannot be turned against Schenker as a criticism. For, as already mentioned in the foreword, in his formulation of the fundamental-line concept, Schenker took a first step along an evolutionary path. To hear Schenker's fundamental line is to feel the pulse of the work of art, to listen to the driving forces in the tonal organism.

[The next two examples should be self-explanatory.]

Example 199. Mozart, Sonata in F Major, K. 332, First Movement

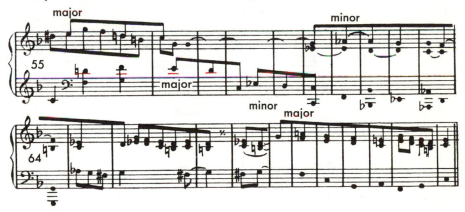

5. In *Harmony*, p. 156, Schenker comments as follows [on two other examples]: "In both cases, is it not the prime contrapuntal principle of voice leading which dominates the development?"

Example 200.   Bach, *WTC I,* Prelude in C Major, BWV 924

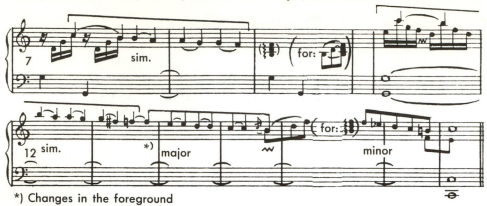

*) Changes in the foreground

Again, listen to the pulsation in the finale of Mozart's *A*-minor sonata [K. 310]; how marvelously it drives forward by means of linkage technique (see chapter 1) after the appoggiatura of bar 4 to ever new formations and expansions.

Linkage technique of the fundamental line *(Urlinienknüpftechnik)*—what an important aid for tonally cohesive organization! First of all, consider examples already cited in the first chapter: Mozart, *D*-minor Fantasy; Beethoven, Sonata op. 110. Now, once again, Mozart's Fantasy in *C* Minor, K. 396:

Example 201.   Mozart, Fantasy in C Minor, K. 396

How clearly Mozart differentiates, by the ligature, the bb^2 from d^3 and c^3 (which are distinguished by wedges)—really as though he wanted to set up the motive for the left hand.[6] (But how completely absent are such interconnections

---

6. Although only the first part of the Fantasy is contained in the manuscript (with, incidentally, an added violin part) and the middle section cited here has come down to us as a completion by Stadler, an at least indirect authorship by Mozart seems to me undeniable.

from the playing of the pianists—how remiss they are in their obligation to the work of art! And when, as a necessary consequence, their playing makes no effect on the listener, they are quick to explain that these compositions no longer correspond to the "consciousness of the times.")

In the finale of his Eighth Symphony, Beethoven sets up a repetition but does not carry it to completion; he saves the completion for the new thematic group:

Example 202.   Beethoven, Eighth Symphony, First Movement

[See the superscripts a), b), a^1), b^1) above the music.]

A comparable example is Chopin's Nocturne in *F*, op. 15 no. 1, where the expected conclusion of the first part finds its realization as the beginning of the middle section. (See example 13.)

"Semper idem sed non eodem modo"—ever the same, but not in the same way. That was the motto that Schenker placed at the front of *Der Tonwille* and, because it is not unrelated, also the second volume of *Kontrapunkt*.[7] Ever the same, simplest, primal event courses through the veins of the work of art, dispensing everlasting life.

As early as the second volume of *Der Tonwille* Schenker arrived at a precise definition of the fundamental-line concept:

> The fundamental line presents the unfolding *(Auswicklung)* of a basic sonority, expressing tonality in the horizontal plane. The tonal system, too, joins in expression of tonality. Its task is to bring a purposeful organization into the world of chords by selecting the scale degrees from among them. The liaison between the horizontal version of tonality through the fundamental line and the vertical through the scale degrees is voice leading.[8] [Compare example 74.]

Later, the individual motions of the fundamental line condensed into linear progressions—that is, passing motions through the fixed diatonic intervals. (See chapter 3, section 2.) And finally, the principle of the ideally sustained head-tone, which is precisely the agent capable of securing coherence and connection between the most distant points,[9] made it possible to draw the individual linear progressions

-----

[7. The same motto headed *Free Composition* as well.]

[8. *Der Tonwille II*, p. 4.]

9. See Mozart, Fantasy in *C* Minor, K. 396:

Example 203. Mozart, Fantasy in C Minor, K. 396

And moreover, Schenker, *Free Composition*, fig. 119, 15, for Brahms, Symphony no. 4, second movement:

Example 204. Brahms, Fourth Symphony, Second Movement (after Schenker, *Free Composition,* fig. 119, 15)

together into a cohesive whole. It caused the linear progressions to be recognized as ever new impulses and unfoldings, behind which stood the ultimate, simplest diatonic fundamental-line progression as a unifying force. The linear progressions of voice leading constitute the strata of the middleground, which connects the background stratum, the fundamental structure, to the foreground, the final manifest appearance of the work.[10] The fundamental line moves, as the original passing event, above the original nature-born and chord-generating scale degrees; together with them, it forms the *fundamental structure.* Schenker's theory of fundamental structure amounts to revelation of the unity of the musical work of art. Without the fundamental structure, there can be no insight into the true synthesis of the masterwork. The fundamental structure alone is the guardian of tonality, and only it can secure unity and coherence regardless of the dimensions involved or the complexity of diminution.

Section 2.   The Fundamental Structure

The composer's business is the composing-out of a sonority. This leads him from a fundamental structure as background through prolongations and diminutions to a foreground structure.[11]

Cohesion is the most important thing in music. But the highest secret of all cohesion is this: *A musical content, which operates in the foreground and is there laid out before us, enters into a state of true cohesion only if it issues from a prior cohesion deep in the background—a cohesion that is sensed in advance in a clairvoyant manner.*[12]

Consider again the model of the divider—example 91—as applied to the fundamental *C:*

Example 205.

Here the triad of nature receives its first, simplest artistic unfolding. In the bass, the fifth-space is shaped into a temporal event by means of arpeggiation;[13] the upper voice, by means of a passing tone, has horizontalized the third-space, making it melodic.

[10. As it is defined in *Free Composition,* the foreground may comprise several (even many) strata close to, but not identical to, the actual surface of the music.]

11. Schenker, *Jahrbuch I,* p. 188.

12. Schenker, *Jahrbuch III,* p. 20. [Emphasis in original.]

13. Schenker calls the image of the bass arpeggiation the "sacred triangle." (See *Free Composition,* §19.)

Now if the e^2, the first fundamental-line tone of the original third-progression, is prolonged by an octave-progression (a downward coupling e^2–e^1), and if d^2, the first passing tone, is prolonged by an upward coupling d^1–d^2 in order to return to c^2, then we obtain the outline of Bach's first Prelude in C Major [of *Well-Tempered Clavier I*]. [This is how the prelude becomes] extended through time from the primal womb of the triad, timeless above all temporal process. (Compare examples 120 and 134.)

The prolongations define *strata (Schichten);* each fundamental-line tone is expanded by elaboration, and each prolonged tone can in turn receive its own prolongations. The fundamental line can be a third-progression, a fifth-progression (as in example 107, Bach's Prelude in Bb), or even an octave progression. In each case, the fundamental structure is the guardian and bearer of tonality. Indeed, only through the fundamental line does the concept of tonality acquire its higher and true meaning as demanding a temporal realization of a *single* sonority. The examples given earlier in connection with chordal arpeggiation may also serve here as reinforcement.

By reason of his long and most intensive study, Schenker also arrived at a perfected graphic representation of his discovery of fundamental line and prolongation; the clearer his insight, the clearer the graphic representation became as well. It is unfortunately impossible to offer complete graphic analyses *(Urlinientafeln)* here. The presentation of Bach's C-Major Prelude comes from Schenker's *Five Graphic Music Analyses*, whose most thorough study cannot be recommended strongly enough. It has been the purpose of the present work above all to acquaint the reader with Schenker's foundational concepts and to motivate further study.

There is a hidden interdependence between the events of the background and those of the foreground. This has been mentioned earlier. (In example 3, the sixteenth-note motion continues unaltered until the motion through the fourth a^2–e^2 is completed.)

In example 162, Mozart begins the development of the sonata with his first motive. This motive is continued—at least in regard to rhythmic structure—until the bass arrives at the decisive passing tone d. At that point the shape of the foreground changes.

The organic growth, from the background, of foreground diminution is vividly illustrated by the first theme [and modulation] from Beethoven's G-Major Sonata, op. 14 no. 2. In the motion toward the second theme group, which is in the dominant, the possibility of parallel fifths arises when the bass moves from G to A on its way to D. These fifths are averted by an anticipating sixth (see chapter 3, section 6):

Example 206.

This underlying motion determines the whole physiognomy of the first theme group. It presents itself first in the neighboring tone e^2 of bar 2—the whole motive-repetition is based on this neighboring tone—; it motivates the additional repetition in bars 6–7. It prevents a definitive closure at the end of the antecedent in bar 8: d^2 is taken up again in the same measure; in the next measure, with the aid of a trill (which itself represents a neighboring-tone motion) it is driven upward to the neighboring tone e^2. (Observe the *cresc.* and *sf.*) The following bar brings an acceleration. In bar 13 there is still another execution of the neighboring tone, [now] in thirty-second notes. In bar 15 the lower voice reaches the divider d, whose third appears in the upper voice as $f\sharp^2$ in bar 17. The *decisive* e^2 of bar 18 is now ornamented by a special appoggiatura (the $f\sharp^2$ repeated from the preceding bar). This appoggiatura is integrated into the diminution—into the sixteenth-notes in bar 20 and the sixteenth-note descent of bars 22ff.—and is continued still further, into the second theme.

Example 207.   Beethoven, Sonata in G Major, op. 14 no. 2

A small seed is sown, and a wonderland of beauty and variety sprouts from it![14]

> That which is motivic in the foreground is independent in appearance only; in fact, it has a perspective, and rests on the narrow shoulders of only a few original intervals of a fundamental structure. . . . *Therefore the entire foreground is a single outpouring of diminution, only a figure.*[15] Where the whole is not a figure in this sense, the motives sound as though snatched from thin air, abrupt, pasted together, like some tasteless bauble.[16]

A neighboring tone also points the way to the structure of Bach's *F*-major fugue, which was presented in example 144. Only now does one understand the relation between the theme of this fugue and the repetition in the large structure.

The following example and discussion are from Schenker's *Jahrbuch II*, p. 41, on Chopin's Nocturne in F♯ Major, op. 15 no. 2:

> The illustration at a) shows the fundamental structure,[17] that at b) the first appearance of the neighboring tone as the first gesture of diminution:

Example 208.   Chopin, Nocturne in F♯ Major, op. 15 no. 2 (after Schenker, *Jahrbuch II*, p. 41)

From this point on, the motive spreads into every blood vessel of the piece. The individual third-progressions, and even the cover tone[18] $c\sharp^2$, are decorated

---

[14. This reading of the bass is preferable to the one by Schenker in *Free Composition*, fig. 47, 2.]

[15. *Figur.* The German word is somewhat more comprehensive than its English cognate.]

16. Schenker, *Jahrbuch II*, p. 40. We have seen the opposite in the masterworks, where even literal "ornaments" are infused with the lifeblood of the fundamental line.

[17. According to the definitions in *Free Composition*, the illustration at a) would be assigned to the middleground strata.]

[18. "A cover tone is a tone of the inner voice which appears above the foreground diminution. It constantly attracts the attention of the ear, even though the essential voice-leading events take place beneath it." (*Free Composition*, p. 107.)]

with the neighboring tone. The cover tone moreover leads a life of its own, which, in summary, appears as follows:

Example 209. Chopin, Nocturne in F♯ Major, op. 15 no. 2 (after Schenker, *Jahrbuch* II, p. 41)

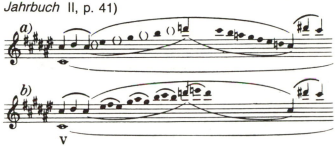

The parallelism $c\sharp^2$–$d\sharp^2$–$c\sharp^2$: $c\sharp^2$–d^3–$c\sharp^2$: $c\sharp^2$–$d\sharp^3$–$c\sharp^3$ etc. betokens a brilliant creative power.

An inner unity of diminution is possible only by virtue of its origin in the maternal womb of the fundamental line. This unity becomes the figure of the whole; it alone is the organic heart of music.

Section 3.   A Brief Look at Formal Organization in Music

Everyone sees the raw material; only those who are able to do something with it find content; and form remains a mystery to most.

For every artwork, large or small, everything depends on the *conception*.

Goethe

Schenker's theory is capable of providing a view of the nature of musical form. [The relevant concepts are] his theory of fundamental structure, which guarantees the unity of the work of art; the fundamental line, which, with its background repetitions, establishes true coherence also in the course of motivic events; and the theory of the foreground as a "figure," which shows that form and content are inseparably connected, and that the living tonal organism cannot be seen as having "kernel" and "outer shell."

The inexhaustible productive power of our masters, their art of improvisation, and their improvisatory art *(ihre Stegreifkunst)* are understandable only in terms of Schenker's theory. The life-giving breath of their formal organization, which seems to capture the work in flight and to invigorate it from inception to completion, can be understood only as a sweep of improvisation.

The natural drive to the fifth, the return from it into the primal womb of the point of origin, the penetration of this force into the flowerings of diminution— this is the spirit of sonata form. Not the lining up of themes, of principal theme and subordinate theme *(Haupt- und Seitensatz)*, as our schematic theory books would have it.

Content becomes palpable as form; through form, it becomes comprehensible. Comprehensibility [springs] from the spirit of association (the law of repetition), [and] from the spirit of our inborn feeling for the strongest overtones.

The simplest formal unit, antecedent-consequent construction, was bequeathed to us already by the simplest linear progression, beginning from the fifth [or third] as head tone and descending first to $\hat{2}$ above V, and its repetition, leading to $\hat{1}$ above I. (See example 103.) The organic growth of such a unit—precisely with the aid of prolongations—constitutes the organic aspect of sonata form. Everything in the sonata strives to secure this formal entity for the whole work, to make it visible to the mind "like a beautiful picture or a comely person." (See the letter by Mozart quoted in chapter 2, section 1.) For this reason the sonata also resists any lining-up of lyrical segments closed within themselves; the lyrical element finds a place here at most as an occasional episode, which signifies only a brief respite from the forward thrust.[19]

Beethoven strives for the most intimate interpenetration of formal parts in his Sonata in *E* Major, op. 109. He integrates the entire second theme into a descending seventh-progression, which is derived from the inversion of the second, $a\sharp^2-b^2$, which is expected:

Example 210.   Beethoven, Sonata in E Major, op. 109

Consider too the profound connection of the first and second themes in Beethoven's Eighth Symphony (example 185), or that in the finale of the same symphony (example 202). If one compares with this, as a counter-example, a work such as Schubert's Sonata in *A* Major, op. 120, one easily sees the crucial difference. In his later sonatas (the *C*-minor!), Schubert tried to abandon this path along which he had been directed by his predominantly lyric genius. On the other hand, what a profound formal instinct Brahms reveals in his Tragic Overture, op. 81: in order to circumvent an exact repetition (a^1-a^2), and yet to avoid simply writing a symphonic first movement, at the repetition [bar 187ff.] he fashions the motive of bars 6–8 (which stems from bars 4–5 [as shown in example 211]) into an episode

19. Brahms to Gustav Jenner, as reported in Jenner's memoirs: "On the other hand, it [sonata form] was cultivated by the great romantics in a lyric spirit that stood in contradiction to its innermost dramatic nature. This contradiction can be sensed even in Schumann." Compare Schenker, *Harmony*, p. 246: "In the form of established keys we have the same step progression, albeit at a superior level. For the sake of the construction of content in a larger sense, the natural element of step progression is elevated correspondingly." [The bracketed interpolation is by the author.]

of its own *(molto più moderato)*. How eerily he moves into this episode by the repetitious stopping in bars 4–6 [of the *molto più moderato*] *(molto p, sempre)*! How marvelously the original shape is regained 46 bars from the end [at bar 384], where bars 17ff. are repeated!

Example 211.   Brahms, *Tragic Overture,* op. 81

In the sonata, the great masters took pains to break up lyrical interludes, wherever they occurred, near the end[20] so as to make them usable for the continuation. Consider, for example, the second themes in the first and last movements of Mozart's *G*-Minor Symphony, or the continuation of the second theme in the Eroica (bar 95ff.).

The concept of the "development" section, and along with it the three-part form a^1 b a^2, is to be explained by the necessity to lead back [to the tonic] from the stabilized, tonicized fifth, the dominant, which, in the foreground, has taken on the *appearance* of a key. The avenue of return was opened with the aid of the passing seventh; expansion and prolongation of this very seventh usually provides the content of the development. The seventh will be expanded by being transformed into a consonant state (see chapter 3, section 4). This is the case, for example, in Beethoven's *G*-Major Sonata, op. 49 no. 2 (see example 161), to cite one among many. Schenker, in his analysis of the *Eroica,* discusses this and also another possibility for providing content:

> As a rule, in order to gain content for the development, a passing seventh that leads back to the recapitulation (V) is composed out in such a way that, as in strict counterpoint, it is presented at first in a consonant state and is then tied over. In the present case, this would appear as follows:

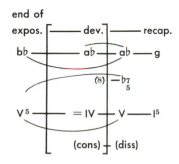

This form of composing-out is impossible, however, when the seventh stands at the beginning of the development, as it does here. As fig. 2 [our example 212] shows, Beethoven here chooses another type of composing-out—

[20. That is, shortly before the lyrical section would have reached its natural point of closure.]

Example 212.   Beethoven, *Eroica* Symphony (after Schenker, *Jahrbuch III*, fig. 3)

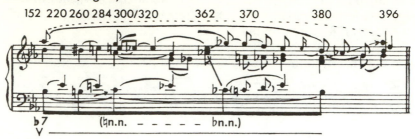

to be precise, a horizontal unrolling of the seventh chord. (Compare, for example, the development of the first movement of Beethoven's op. 81a.) Against this seventh-progression he sets in the bass a counterpoint that describes a neighboring-tone motion.[21]

In minor-key works, when the exposition moved only as far as the third (III), the necessity of leading onward to the fifth (V) provided the opportunity for a middle section. (See Mozart, *A*-Minor Sonata, example 162.) If the exposition itself moved to the fifth (V), but with a minor third, this minor triad had to be converted into a major triad usable for the return to I (chapter 1, section 6). This could be accomplished by composing out a neighboring tone, for example, as happens for a different reason in example 143. (Compare also Haydn, Sonata in *E* Minor [Hob. 34], bars 26ff. of the development.)[22]

Yet this listing by no means exhausts all of the possible varieties. One need only consider the paths that lead first of all to the lower fifth, the subdominant. (See above, example 70!)[23]

On connection in tonal space: consider, for example, the *F*-Major Sonata [K. 332] by Mozart; c^3, from which an octave coupling (consisting of *c–g* in the first theme group and *g–c* in the second) descends, reappears at the end of the first part[24] as head-tone once again. At the end of the development, it is led to bb^2, and finally, in the recapitulation, progresses to its conclusion in the last large fifth-progression. (See example 110.)

On connection by means of fundamental-line motives: which "form textbook" speaks of them? and who shows interconnections as Schenker does:

In the development section of the first movement of Beethoven's Sonata op. 109, the composer establishes the following high points:

---

21. *Jahrbuch III*, p. 43f. [Example 212 is actually excerpted from Schenker's fig. 3.]
[22. Bars 72ff. of the complete movement.]
[23. A fuller discussion of the possible coordinations of sonata form with tonal structure is provided by Ernst Oster's editorial commentary in *Free Composition*, pp. 139–141.]
[24. I.e., the exposition.]

Example 213a.

The manner in which Beethoven suddenly abandons the high $g\sharp^3$ in bar 21 and jumps down to $d\sharp^2$ has puzzled everyone. What could this leap, this abrupt change, signify? Even if we achieved the insight that a relation exists between these two widely separated points—that, indeed, the compositional idea is to move up from $g\sharp^3$ (which is to become the head-tone of the reprise) to b^3—we still would not have gained the ultimate clarity. The latter is provided by the following relations:

Example 213b.

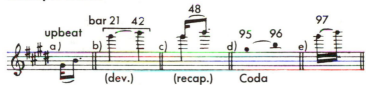

The improvisational fantasy of the master pursues both tones of the upbeat even in the development and the coda! He must drive after them. They signify a motive to him—the key to a world of unity and coherence. But what does the theory of sonata form care about such a miracle? And yet, the substance of this movement develops only through this miracle.[25]

The masters succeed also in achieving unity in the rondo form, which, because of its frequent repetitions (a b a c a b a), can easily become monotonous and sectionalized. Who would guess, for example, that in Beethoven's Sonata in $E\flat$ Major, op. 7, the c-minor middle episode is already predestined in the eighth-note appoggiatura c^3 of bar 10? (Observe the crescendo and the staccato sixteenths leading up to it, and the $sf!$) And how marvelously Brahms integrates the middle part of the rondo in the last movement of his Cello Sonata in F, op. 99. The head of the theme is repeated, hesitatingly and in enlargement, on $g\flat$:[26]

[25. Schenker, "Organic Structure in Sonata Form," trans. by Orin Grossman, in Maury Yeston, ed., *Readings in Schenker Analysis and Other Approaches* (New Haven: Yale University Press, 1977), pp. 48–50. Translation modified somewhat.]

[26. Bar 54 of the movement. The figure that is enlarged beginning on $g\flat$ (see the brackets in example 214) represents the head of the theme in its rhythmic aspect only. The enlargement (bars 4–5 of the example) has a more specific pitch relationship to the model three bars earlier in that the first three notes of each move through a third-space. The curly brackets in example 214 show merely that the cello's descending third f–$e\flat$–$d\flat$ is continued in the piano by another descending third (departing from the cello's final note) as an accompanying inner voice in parallel sixths below the theme; this new accompanying voice thus

Example 214. Brahms, Violoncello Sonata in F Major, op. 99, Rondo

The middle section (*bb* minor) follows; I will not go into its relationship [to the rest of the movement] here, but it leads once again to the enlarged thematic head on *gb*. Further still: the *gb* even precipitates the beginning of the reprise on *Gb*.[27] Where is "formalism" in this? In any event, this way of shaping a rondo is more brilliant and—yes—more *original* than practically everything written since Brahms.

The concept of variation as an art is completely unthinkable without the concept of a fundamental structure and the craving for diminution. This artistic form was handed down to our classical masters as a legacy from C. P. E. Bach's inexhaustible art of variation.[28] Binding variations together by motivic means also benefits the unity of the work. Accordingly, Brahms obtains the appoggiatura motive in the third variation of his Handel Variations, op. 24, from the completion of the otherwise incomplete scalar descent that ends the preceding variation:

Example 215a. Brahms, Variations on a Theme by Handel, op. 24

Brahms also uses a similar linkage technique in other small pieces which, although complete in themselves, combine to form a larger entity, as for example in the Waltzes op. 39:

Example 215b. Brahms, Waltzes op. 39

grows directly out of the cello's descending third. The dotted slurs indicate a relationship between the two important formal points with which they are associated: bb–db^1 at the beginning of the episode, db^2–bb^2 at the beginning of the restatement on Gb.]

[27. Bar 85 of the movement.]

[28. See especially C. P. E. Bach, *Kurze und leichte Klavierstücke mit veränderten Reprisen*, edited, with explanatory comments, by Oswald Jonas; Universal Edition no. 13311.]

(Unfortunately space does not permit a description of the elegant manner in which Chopin, in his waltzes—especially the *F*-major of op. 34 and the *A*♭-major op. 42—, creates a cohesive, inimitable work of art from a series of small waltzes apparently only loosely connected with one another.)

Finally, even the fugue becomes a work of art only when a unifying tonal framework *(Satz)* stands behind all of its foreground voice leading. Compare the process of arpeggiation in Bach's *C*-minor Fugue as presented in chapter 2, section 2; see also example 144. And the "rule" according to which the *dux* in a [tonal] fugue must be altered to form the *comes* (see example 216) takes on deep meaning only when it is understood as a unifying force that unites two otherwise merely juxtaposed "themes."[29]

Example 216. Bach, *WTC I*, Fugue in F Major

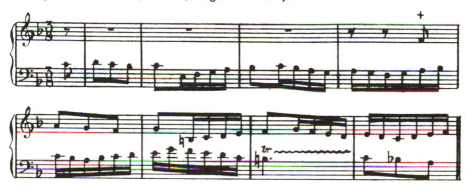

Two quotations from Schenker may bring our journey through his work to a close.

> A new concept and mode of presentation must be established—very different from that of the analyses that remain bound to the surface—if we are to succeed in tracing foreground relationships to their origin in the background and middleground. But this new mode must not be called analysis, if that term is also to be applied to what is set to paper by all too many others. Only such a clear differentiation could finally impress upon music lovers, who without hesitation tend to equate their sensibilities with those of the masters, that their sensibilities are by no means of such a high order; that

---

[29. *Dux* and *comes* are of course two different aspects of the same theme. Evidently the intended meaning here is *thematic entrances*. In example 216, and generally, the unifying force of the "rule" of the tonal answer consists in reshaping the theme for the *comes* aspect so that its beginning is integrated into the composed-out tonic triad; in this way the tonic is retained and confirmed more clearly and the tonicization of the fifth is embedded within the answer rather than occurring abruptly at its beginning. This avoids an undesirable sectionalization.]

on the contrary, they are vastly inferior to the sensibilities of musicians who, without wishing or being able to compare themselves with the masters, nevertheless show themselves to be more gifted in their sensitivity to the synthesis of genius.[30]

Those who are able to hear the whole *from* the whole—how they would rejoice at the radiance of improvisatory fantasy, for example even in the last string quartets and symphonies of Beethoven, which overshadows all melody. Beethoven remained until his last breath—to adapt an expression of Hölderlin's—an emissary of gushing sound, a prophet of tone-totality whose creations are graced by light and resiliency.[31]

---

30. *Jahrbuch III*, p. 101.

31. *Jahrbuch II*, p. 54.

Appendix A

The Relation of Word and Tone

Section 1. Language Rhythm and Musical Rhythm

Before we begin to investigate how word and tone can be brought together in an artistic manner we must first reconsider the basic problem of rhythm *(Rhythmus)*. We discover there a marvelous parallelism and a strong similarity between the principles that guide the poet in his handling of poetic meter and those that guide the composer in his handling of musical meter. In both cases, it is not merely the sense of rhythm that bespeaks special gifts; it is, rather, the ability to perceive the basic temporal unit *(Grundmass)* behind the most diversified [surface] configuration *(Gestaltung)* and to avoid going astray. The simple and ungifted person perceives rhythm *(Rhythmus)* only through strict "scansion," so to speak, and becomes irritated when the accent determined by poetic content (the meaning-accent)[1] fails to coincide with the accent produced by scansion. The artist, on the contrary, by virtue of his artistic capacity, finds just here the strongest stimulus for creation *(Gestaltung)*. Thus Goethe writes, in the great elegy,[2]

Wĭe léicht ŭnd zíerlĭch, klár ŭnd zárt gĕwóbĕn
Schwĕbt, séră̆phgléich, aŭs érnstĕr Wólkĕn Chór,
Ăls glích ĕs íhr, ă̆m bláuĕnÁthĕr dróbĕn
Ĕin schlánk Gĕbíld aŭs líchtĕm Dúft ĕmpór!

[1. *Gestalteter Akzent (Sinnakzent).*]
[2. The "Marienbad Elegy," written in the 1820s. The translations provided in this appendix do not in general correspond to the German original with respect to prosody or word-placement.]

How light and graceful, clear and tender wove,
From choirs of clouds a seraph comes to view,
As though like her, from gentle haze above,
A slender form emerging in the blue!

The meter is iambic; the meaning-accent coincides with the metric accent. At least up to a certain point. At the beginning of the second line, Goethe places the word *schwebt* (floats) on the arsis. Because of the impetus of the meter, whose effect continues as if automatically, we want to move ahead quickly and read further: but the meaning of the word deters us; we hesitate, and the word literally comes to a halt: it "floats," and takes on form. Observe too the comma, and how it conforms to the poet's intention. Now would one say that Goethe has here changed his meter? Is it not far more correct to sense the manner in which he has arrived at such delicate differentiations and poetic forms for his language and thoughts [precisely] from the constancy of the meter? or [as another example], he begins his poem *"Vermächtnis"* as follows:

Kĕin Wésĕn kánn zŭ níchts zĕrfállĕn!

The first word holds such power that we naturally understand it first as a thesis, and emphasize it in reading and reciting; only as we read further do we become oriented with respect to the real metric organization. How much more forcefully the word *kein* strikes the ear, in agreement with the deep meaning of the poem.

Now, one final example: How closely the representation in the following (from Goethe, *"Pandora,"* line 155ff.) corresponds to the actual events depicted:

Dĕr Fáckĕl Flámmĕ, mórgĕndlích dĕm Stérn vŏrán
Ĭn Vátĕrhändĕn áufgĕschwúngĕn, kündĕst dú
Tăg vór dĕm Tágĕ! Göttlích wérdĕ dú vĕréhrt.
. . . .
Dĕswégĕn ích dĕr Ábĕndáschĕ héil'gĕn Schátz
Ĕntblóssĕnd früh zŭ néuĕm Glúttrieb áufgĕfácht,
Vŏrléuchtĕnd méinĕm wáckĕrn árbĕitstréuĕn Vólk.

Flame of the torch, lifted by morning to the stars
in fatherly hands, thou proclaimest
day before day. Be thou revered as a god.

Baring the ember, the scared treasure left from evening,
I early stirred it to new fervor
to light the way for my brave and industrious people.

How clearly the poet literally *anticipates* the metric accent with the meaning-accent in the third and sixth lines! How supple his expression of the meaning![3]

Don't we see in this process a relationship very similar to the one we observed earlier with respect to rhythm? Poetic meter and form generating flexibility on the one side, musical meter and compositional shaping on the other. How should the composer proceed in setting measured texts? In the light of the above comparison, can there be any doubt? Artistic declamation will consist of this: musical meter is to be placed in correspondence to poetic meter, and the deviations of emphasis that result from meaning are to be musically represented, composed-out, but with *musical* resources rather than with rhythmic ones. It is nothing but a sign of the complete decline of musical creative power when modern composers renounce this form of declamation and espouse another as the only true and possible one. They claim that the declamation of the old composers was "contrary to the meaning" *(sinnwidrig);* here they forget just one thing: that their way of working has to be called "contrary to art" *(kunstwidrig)*.[4] Once again we find that conceited boasting about the natural sense of rhythm that we saw earlier among the theorists, who also chase after the accent produced by composing-out (meaning-accent) with their barlines and achieve a complete state of rhythmic disorder.[5]

As a most general principle, then: musical meter corresponds to the structure of the poetic line, regardless of any deviation within the line, whether it be the setting of a meaning-emphasized word on the arsis or—the opposite—an unemphasized word on the thesis. Emphasis through meaning coincides with the musical composing-out. The classicists adhered closely to this principle—both Schubert, whose lieder derive their marvelous power of expression above all from their

---

[3. In contrast to the accents of the iambic meter, the meaning accents fall on *Tag* (day) in the third line and on the prefix *vor* (before, in advance) in the sixth. In standard speech, too, the prefix *vor* would receive the accent in *vorleuchtend*.]

[4. This is no doubt directed against Wolf and his partisans, among others. A patronizing attitude toward Schubert, in particular, was clearly expressed in 1907 by Ernest Newman in *Hugo Wolf* (second edition, New York: Dover Publications, 1966): "Like Mozart, [Schubert] was a little too fluent; the music came out of him rather too easily for it always to come from a very great depth. His poetic sense was often at fault. . . . He was not always careful to think out a poem as a whole, and to find a fresh expression for each fresh emotional point in it; he was often too content with the lazy strophic form, either repeating his music mechanically in different verses, or merely altering it according to a few easy formulas. . . ." (p. 154).]

5. Brahms's opinion of this effort of Riemann's is shown in a letter to Simrock, in which he gives vent to his disapproval: "We always phrase and mark as our classicists did. Not only do we get along well enough with this method: we find nothing left to be desired, in spite of the fact that we don't think about phrases and the like so cleverly as Herr R. [!] And we have no cause to do away with the bar line—Herr R. should have the courage to do so, if he wants to be *consistent.*" [The bracketed exclamation mark is by the author.]

profoundly shaped declamation, and Brahms. Only a declining artistic instinct, and ultimately the complete absence of such instinct, could see in this procedure "naiveté and inattentiveness among the venerable old composers" and vainly claim that the other procedure—in truth a vacuously naturalistic one—represented progress.

In the theater, which demands greater clarity and a stronger emphasis of the meaning-accent to make the action understandable, such declamation was perhaps appropriate. That is to say, the libretto itself had to achieve the closest possible correspondence between meaning-accent and metric accent. This, to be sure, did not exactly enhance its poetic quality; but it did make the libretto more useful as a point of departure for the theater composer. The Wagnerian type of declamation, too, is to be understood only in the light of its theatrical purpose. It served the purpose of clarity, and often approached speech-song *(Sprechgesang)*, in which word and meaning are the decisive elements. And Wagner frequently had to handle declamation in a different way by reason of instrumentation; for example, he might delay the entry of the voice in order to avoid covering it with an overly powerful sound. But to transplant this type of declamation to the lied, as happened after Wagner (similarly to his other compositional principles and his treatment of the orchestra), and to regard this as a step forward in lied composition—this could occur only in an era that was no longer equal to artistic synthesis and tried to mask its inadequacy through superficial measures.

For Schubert in his *Müller* songs, the following treatment of the text is self-evident.

Example 217.   Schubert, *Die schöne Müllerin*, no. 2, "Wohin?"

Ich   hört ein Bächlein   rau-schen wohl   aus dem Fel – sen – – quell

The composing-out, the arpeggiation, ensures that we perceive the beginning of the [second] verse-line clearly, and that we do not hear d^1 in bar 3 as a principal tone, in spite of the fact that it occurs on the strong beat in correspondence with the poetic meter.

Schubert basically adheres strictly to this principle. He deviates from it only in the rarest cases (in all twenty-four songs of *Die Winterreise* only four times, and only twice in the twenty songs of *Die schöne Müllerin*), and there are always important reasons behind those deviations. In *"Gefrorene Tränen"* (*Die Winterreise*, D. 911, no. 4) we find:

Example 218a.   Schubert, *Die Winterreise*, no. 3, "Gefrorne Thränen"

–ab: ob   es mir denn   ent – – gan – – gen, dass

Schubert had first written in the manuscript, in accordance with the poetic meter:

Example 218b.

He then made the improvement contained in the final version. It is certain that not only the meaning of the line played a role in his alteration, but also the constellation of the accompaniment with its imitative entrances.

In lied composition, too, we see that for the masters, composing-out is the central matter. Through composing-out, they were able to cope with any possible non-alignment of metric accent and meaning-accent. Every Schubert lied offers examples of this. A single example, typical of many, may show how composing-out together with the obligation of artistic declamation can do justice to the most profound psychological demands. In his *"Lied der Mignon"* [D. 877, no. 4], Schubert presents three different declamations of the same line—precisely through composing-out—while maintaining the same metric placement:

Example 219.   Schubert, "Lied der Mignon," D. 877 no. 4

In the first setting, the concept of *Sehnsucht* (longing) stands in the foreground of emphasis, in agreement with the simple metric accent, as though the concept were being introduced for the first time. The second form already makes it clear that the degree of our familiarity *(Kenntnis)* with this concept is of importance. Here the word *kennt* (knows) is itself kept at a high pitch-level, even if only in the form of a sustained appoggiatura. In the third setting, passionately explosive in effect, Schubert leads the fifth on up to the neighboring tone *f,* which now places *kennt* at the apex of the bar. Unfortunately our discussion must for lack of space be limited to this one example. But attention should be drawn also to the two different placements of emphasis in Schubert's *"Rückblick"* from *Die Winterreise,* at the words *"auf meinen Hut";* this change of emphasis gives expression so splendidly to the confusion that afflicts the wretched speaker, pursued from all sides and sinking into madness. (Compare also in Brahms, *Lieder und Gesänge* op. 57 no. 2, the settings of the words *"Dieser ungemessnen Glut."*)

All of this is the yield of composing-out, which has the power to bring out critical points of expression and meaning without ignoring the basic rhythmic accent.

Section 2.   The Musical Representation of a Text

In spite of the fact that music holds no direct association with nature, by virtue of its inner logic, which it acquired in the course of its development as an art, it can do justice even to the artistic representation *(Gestaltung)* of a text. Such a representation *(Gestalten)* will be artistically potent—that is to say, it will deserve to be called a representation—only if the desired effect is sought by purely musical means rather than by superficially evocative ones, such as mere imitation of movement or even noise-like sound effects. Only then will the creative process *(Gestaltung)* incorporate and reflect psychological necessity. The individual tone must be subjected, within the tonal organism, to an experience similar to that expressed in the language. Let us return first to example 163. A single word there takes on tangible shape. But note well: this shaping is possible only within and under the assumption of the chord of nature and its unfolding through voice leading. The principle of necessity that resides in the nature-given system is also a precondition for the following example:

Example 220.   Schubert, *Schwanengesang,* no. 5, "Aufenthalt"

Instead of leading *e* to *d♯*, Schubert first "freezes" the tone in the guise of *eb*,[6] in combination with the *c* that is prefixed to *b* in the bass. The *eb* must first be transformed into *d♯* above *b* before it can return to *e*.

Handel achieves a similar effect in a similar way—here it is even embedded in an extended linear progression—in the following passage:

Example 221.   Handel, *Samson,* Act II: "Return, Return, Oh God of Hosts," bars 38–42

[6. ". . . *lässt den Ton zum 'es' erstarren*"—the "immobilization" of the *d♯* as *eb* reflects the *strarrender Fels* of the text.]

Again it should be emphasized that such effects are unattainable unless they rest on the foundation of voice leading and tonal system.

An approximate assessment of the full significance of voice leading and its linear progressions for the representation of language can be gained from the next example. Schubert was confronted with the following difficult task in setting the second stanza of the poem *"Wehmut"* by Collin:

Denn was in Winde tönend weht,
Was aufgetürmt gen Himmel steht,
Und auch der Mensch, so hold vertraut
Mit all' der Schönheit, die er schaut,
Entschwindet und vergeht.

For all that stands singing in the wind,
All that towers upward toward the heavens,
And man too, so graciously at one
With all the beauty that he beholds,
Fades away and vanishes.

With an incomparable stroke of genius, Schubert sets the tripartite subject within a passing motion prolonging V, in order to reach *d* only at the word *entschwindet* (fades away). By means of this fourth-progression in the bass, he secures a unification of the text even stronger than the linguistic one that is sensed in reading; and he even finds time for a lyric mixture (*g–g♯*) at *vertraut* and *Schönheit*.

Example 222.   Schubert, "Wehmut," D. 772

It is only possible to touch upon all of these problems. But it must be said that the present era has forgotten how to see such problems at all and to become conscious of them. It lacks the will to formation *(Gestalt)* and probably also the ability.

In Goethe's sonnet *"Die Liebende schreibt"* the first two stanzas show a certain variance in their third and fourth lines:

> Wer davon hat wie ich gewisse Kunde,
> Mag dem was anders wohl erfreulich scheinen?
> . . . .
> Und immer treffen sie auf jene Stunde,
> Die einzige; da fang' ich an zu weinen.

> For one who has, like I, definite knowledge of those things,
> Could anything else be found delightful?
> . . . .
> And they always touch upon that hour,
> The only one; then I begin to weep.

These two stanzas are the first stanza-pair of the sonnet; their rhymes call for a strophic treatment in the music—that is, the two stanzas want to be set as similarly as possible. But how would it be possible for the musical setting to reflect the fact that the beginning of the fourth line of the second stanza is connected in thought and language to the third line?[7] It would seem almost impossible to give this relationship its proper due with purely musical means. And yet Brahms (who incidentally has here composed a "musical sonnet" without violating the requirements of musical form) accomplishes it, with the aid of an expansion. In essence, then, he does the same thing as the poet, who also carries his thought, his sentence, forward into the following line:

[7. *Die einzige* (the only one) is in apposition to *jene Stunde* of the preceding line.]

Example 223. Brahms, "Die Liebende schreibt," op. 47 no. 5

wie ich ge-wis - se Kun-de, mag dem was an - ders wohl

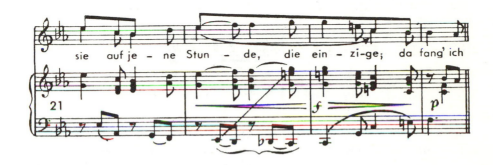

sie auf je - ne Stun - de, die ein - zi-ge; da fang' ich

The neighboring tone c^2 is built into an arpeggiation of the C triad in the second stanza; the passing motion of the upper voice, eb–db–c, is moved forward one bar and placed in the bass (precisely to enhance the C triad). The bb^1, formerly the fifth of eb, now appears in passing as a seventh, coming from c. The rhyme is maintained [musically] (eb^2). The high position of eb^2 is surpassed by the still higher g^2 at *die einzige!*

Mendelssohn, who composed the poem in a freer way, handles this place no less brilliantly than Brahms. At *die einzige* he has the vocal part sustain gb^2; the piano states the motive, and the voice, in imitating it, finds the path for its continuation just at the syllables *"zige."* [See the brackets in example 224.] He joins the tones of these last two syllables with what follows also by means of the portato indication! (Note the crescendo as well.) The tone db^2, the fifth of the harmony in the original motive, even becomes an accented passing tone here—in spite of the semicolon! Thus Mendelssohn, like the poet, ties the beginning of the fourth line motivically (in "meaning") to what precedes it, but in terms of voice leading ("syntactically") to what follows it!

Example 224. Mendelssohn, "Die Liebende schreibt," op. 86 no. 3

und im-mer treffen sie auf je-ne Stunde,   die ein - - - -

zi - - ge; da fang ich

In setting a complete poem to music, the composer must always seek to take advantage of conceptual associations for the benefit of formal associations in the music, which do not always correspond to the form (the stanzas) of the poem. Music, which has greater need of these formal associations, often will not easily relinquish a repetition of the beginning, which will produce a three-part form (a^1–b–a^2). The composer must penetrate deeply into the poem in order to search out those points at which a repetition is suitable.

Thus Schubert, in his lied *"Täuschung"* (*Die Winterreise*, no. 19) establishes a connection between the first line of the first stanza, *Ein Licht tanzt freundlich vor mir her,* and the fourth line of the second stanza, *ihm weist ein helles, warmes Haus* (*Das licht* is conceptually the subject of the verb *weist*), and just here—in the middle of the sentence!—he closes the circle of the three-part form! It is true that a stropic treatment would have been impossible also because the second stanza is lengthened by two lines.

One sees in Mendelssohn's charming lied *"Lieblingsplätzchen"* (op. 99 no. 3) how a three-part form arises from purely verbal/conceptual associations. And Brahm's duet *"Klänge"* (op. 66 no. 2) should be studied in this connection. The poem has two stanzas; the second corresponds to the first in imagery, but surpasses it in spiritual content—and the music is able to reflect this! See also the lied *"Eine gute, gute Nacht"* (op. 59 no. 6).

Wherever possible, our masters preferred strophic form. This may have been because they took delight in accounting for any poetic variants from stanza to stanza by means of variants in the composing-out. How well Brahms adjusts his setting to the content of the poems in his lieder (both of which have two stanzas) *"Dein blaues Auge"* (op. 59 no. 8) and *"Sapphische Ode"* (op. 94 no. 4)! In the two-stanza lied *"O kühler Wald"* (op. 72 no. 3) Brahms alters the beginning of the second stanza: *"Im Herzen tief, da rauscht der Wald!"*. At the words *Im Herzen tief* (deep within my heart) he changes the neighboring tone *g* to *gb*, and expands it into a *Gb* harmony, which he then composes-out as the introduction (see the bass arpeggiation) that is due at this point. The introduction is thus enlarged, the textual entry referred to occurs simultaneously above it. Only at the words *rauscht der Wald* (the forest murmurs) is there a correspondence to the beginning of the first stanza; it is now expressed in terms of motivic and strophic form as well as of language and content. The attenuation of the line that resulted from relocating the words *Im Herzen tief*[8] is compensated by repetition [of *da rauscht der Wald*]. How supple the adaptation of the music to the most refined impulses in the poem—all of which is possible only because the composer felt obliged and bound by the formal idea!

Example 225. Brahms, "O külher Wald," op. 72 no. 3

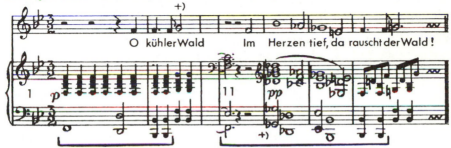

(In Brahm's lied *"Therese"* (op. 86 no. 1), the poet presents the third stanza, in a deliberately roguish way, without relation to the first two, almost as a jest. Brahms does justice to this by composing the third stanza within the expected *B* triad above a repetition of the introduction, as though the poem were already finished and it were left up to the music to provide the answer to the "question" [i.e., the *Frage* mentioned in the first stanza]). In terms of their technique the last two examples bring us close to the song of all songs. The art with which Schubert achieves a strophic songform in *"Der Lindenbaum"* (*Die Winterreise*, no. 5) in spite of seemingly almost insurmountable difficulties is unique in the song literature. The poem is quoted below in its entirety for easy reference:

Am Brunnen vor dem Tore, da steht ein Lindenbaum;
Ich träumt' in seinem Schatten so manchen süssen Traum.
Ich schnitt in seine Rinde so manches liebe Wort;
Es zog in Freud' und Leide zu ihm mich immer fort.

Ich musst' auch heute wandern vorbei in tiefer Nacht,
Da hab' ich noch im Dunkel die Augen zugemacht.

[8. *Vorausschickung der ersten drei Worte.* If the second stanza were exactly parallel to the first, the three words would have appeared after *rauscht der Wald*. Since they are moved forward, and since the musical "stanza" begins, as explained, only at *rauscht der Wald*, the text remaining in the line is shorter by two iambic feet.]

Und seine Zweige rauschten, als riefen sie mir zu:
Komm' her zu mir Geselle, hier find'st du deine Ruh!

Die kalten Winde bliesen mir grad' ins Angesicht,
Der Hut flog mir vom Kopfe, ich wendete mich nicht.
Nun bin ich manche Stunde entfernt von jenem Ort,
Und immer hör' ich's rauschen: du fändest Ruhe dort!

By the well before the gate there stands a lime-tree;
in its shade I dreamt many a sweet dream.
In its bark I carved many a word of love;
in joy as in sorrow I felt ever drawn to it.

Today I had to wander past it at dead of night,
and even in the darkness I closed my eyes.
And its branches rustled as if they were calling to me
'Friend, come here to me—Here you will find rest.'

The cold winds blew straight into my face,
my hat flew from my head—but I did not turn round.
Now I am many hours' journey away from that place;
but I always hear the rustling: 'There you would find rest!'

The contrast of happy recollection and harsh reality permeates all stanzas of the poem. The tenderness *(Lieblichkeit)* of the first stanza, its deep yearning, can, it is true, be placed in correspondence to the third and fourth lines of the outer two stanzas. But how can justice be done to the deep melancholy *(Wehmut)* at the beginning of the second stanza (where the ordeal of reality first begins), or the awesome intensification at the beginning of the third stanza—all within the format of a strophic song?

Schubert precedes his lied with an introduction that consists of two elements: the murmur of the sixteenth-note triplets and the yearning effect of the neighboring-tone motion *c♯–b*.[9] In bar 4 the neighboring tone occurs in the bass, and in the next bar it grows into a complete harmony before returning to *b* at bar 7. The neighboring-tone motion appears again at *So manches liebe Wort* (!), and immediately after in the piano as an echo. For the beginning of the second stanza Schubert finds the inflection to minor adequate to his needs. Only the first four bars of the introduction are repeated, with the neighboring tone of the bass immediately in the low register (!). At the third line Schubert returns to major.

And now the event of the third stanza! Beneath the triplets the bass enters immediately with *C* as an appoggiatura to *B*. The following measures now present an enormous expansion and composing-out of the neighboring tone, as an enlargement of the introduction whose repetition is due;[10] this passage ends with the

---

9. Schubert writes *c♯* in the manuscript with a staccato dot, not with the usual slur to *b*. [The first edition, however, shows the slur, and the proofs were read by the composer.]

10. Schubert does not cancel the sharps of the key signature before the third stanza as he does before the second!

introduction's concluding gesture. How the throbbing of the portato *C* [of bars 50 and 52] is echoed by the portato *B* [of bar 56]! And above this enlarged introduction: the two first lines of the third stanza! The beginning of the song proper can now follow immediately with the third line. The two concluding lines naturally have to be repeated as a result; but how well this repetition—a product of necessity in the first place!—fits the content of the poem. *Und immer hör ich's rauschen* . . . ("but I always hear the rustling . . ."). The introduction, with its turn to the tonic at the close, appears at the end in the manner of a consoling reverberation.

Example 226. Schubert, *Die Winterreise,* no. 4, "Der Lindenbaum"

Appendix B

Schenker's Editorial Work and the Vienna Photostat Archive

Schenker dedicated his life to the understanding of the musical masterwork. His efforts were concerned not merely with the content, however, but also with the external form. The necessity of such concern will be clear to anyone who has once compared a conventional or so-called "instructive" edition of one of the masters with the first edition or, better still, with the manuscript. The editing of musical works has been infiltrated by an insidious practice that, to put it mildly, has to be described as a great nuisance. The reasons for this have been in part to fill the needs of the student, who allegedly wants more detailed performance indications; also in part to feed the vanity of editors who imagine that they know more than the composers *(Besserwisserei)*; and finally, not least, to satisfy the profit motives of business-hungry publishers. Thus the text of a masterwork becomes covered over, as if by a film that distorts the original form to the point of unrecognizability. Moreover, the potential for error in bringing a musical work into print is significantly greater than that for a literary work because of the lack of unambiguous verbal meanings. Since the production of an error-free musical text is a difficult task even with the deepest knowledge and integrity *(bei bestem Wissen und Gewissen)*, one can form an approximate picture of the situation at hand. Schenker continually referred to the importance of *manuscripts*. In all of his editorial work he constantly sought to give proper attention to the original form. His editions of the sonatas of C. P. E. Bach and of J. S. Bach's Chromatic Fantasy and Fugue, and his analytical editions of the last sonatas of Beethoven as well as the text-editions of the complete set, are therefore exemplary. Beyond this, in his analyses of Beethoven's Third, Fifth, and Ninth Symphonies, of Mozart's *g*-minor Symphony, of Chopin études and of numerous other pieces, he provided accurate descriptions of the original manuscripts and of deviations in the first printings. It turned out that the manuscripts show refinements of notation that have not been grasped by any engraver or proofreader—particular details which themselves stand in a secret relationship to the content of the work and which reveal ways of understanding that content which have remained completely unnoticed up to the present time. Subtleties that are not reflected either in the first editions or, for the most part, in the complete and *Urtext* editions based upon them. The masters were so constantly at odds with their publishers over the most primitive errors and distortions of the correct text that they had no opportunity to complain about other matters. Beethoven's letters on this subject are well known. But even Haydn wrote in 1789 to Artaria, "it is a continual annoyance to me that *not a single work* put out under your supervision is free of error."

About these refinements of notation, Schenker wrote as follows in his analytical edition of Beethoven's op. 101:

> The rise and fall of the lines: here they ascend from the lower staff to the upper, there they descend from the upper to the lower. The meaningful interplay of the beams: they reveal to the eye what is happening in the inner world of the tones—here the desire to belong together, there the need to be separated. The secret eloquence of the slurs: uniting those things that belong together in spite of beams or bar lines; separating, in order to make room for counterforces; frequently counteracting each other simultaneously in different time-spans—in performing all of these functions, they present a picture of cultivated and thoroughgoing regularity in the organization of the parts and of the whole. The differentiation of upward and downward stem direction: it makes us perceive the notes as actors in dialog with one another, [clearly delineated in their collaborating or contrasting roles, most beautifully of all] in those places where, for example, a downward stemming so dynamically presages, far in advance, the counterplay of an upward-stemmed series of tones (or vice versa).[1]

Since Schenker fought tirelessly against the besmirching of masterworks by corrupt editions—see, for example, his essay *"Weg mit dem Phrasierungsbogen"* ("Down with the Phrasing Slur") in the first *Jahrbuch*—, since he always emphasized the importance of manuscripts, he was particularly gratified to find a man who had the enthusiasm and, moreover, the material resources necessary to initiate a project that truly must be called a rescue mission for musical culture. Anthony van Hoboken, a Dutch musician and pupil of Schenker's, founded a "Photostat Archive for Musical Manuscripts" at the Austrian National Library. The mission of this archive is to reproduce all obtainable manuscripts of the masters, whether in public or private ownership, and thus to make them generally accessible and to preserve them for posterity. The curatorial board consisted of Professor Robert Haas, director of the Music Division, van Hoboken, and Schenker. At present the collection numbers far more than 30,000 pages, mostly from the holdings of the Paris Conservatoire, the British Museum, the Austrian National and Vienna

---

1. *Beethoven, Sonata A Dur, op. 101,* second edition, p. 4. [The bracketed passage does not appear in the *Einführung,* probably through oversight.]

City Libraries, and the Prussian National Library. It includes Bach's *Well-Tempered Clavier* in three manuscripts; countless works by Handel; sonatas, symphonies, chamber music, oratorios and operas by C. P. E. Bach, Haydn, Mozart, Beethoven and Schubert; many of Schubert's lieder, including the complete *Die Winterreise* and *Schwanengesang;* a major portion of Chopin's works; and many works of Brahms.

Whoever dedicates himself to the study of manuscripts not only will be unable to overlook the magical quality that they exude, but will gain insight into the nature of musical coherence. It is not least of all our masters' manner of writing that convinces us of the profound truth of the Schenkerian theory of unity and of the organic nature of the musical work of art.

In the Sonata op. 101, second movement, Beethoven writes the slurs beginning in bar 30 as follows:

Example 227.   Beethoven, Sonata in A Major, op. 101, Second Movement

How clearly he emphasizes the three-tone motive with its imitations; his placement of the slur across the full half-measure at bar 36 (note also the sextolets in the bass) acts as a signal of the forthcoming rhythmic change: it prepares the motive of the following bar.

The original edition already bypasses this delicacy and places the slurs over the half-measure from bar 30 on. Because of the ties from the second to the third quarters of the bars, this difference may seem unimportant to many; but in performance, the hand will make a different motion to realize Beethoven's intention. Perhaps a proper reverence for meticulous care on the part of the genius—how thoroughly his hearing penetrates into his style of writing!—will rekindle a reverence for tonal life in general. And perhaps the revelation of this scrupulousness may cure many of the absurd notion that the marking of a work for performance can be accomplished better by someone other than its creator.

The effect is perfectly *demonic* where Chopin, in the third bar from the end of the *Berceuse*, writes as follows:

Example 228.   Chopin, Berceuse

Here it is made perceptible to the eye that the third of the tonic, which has always drifted upward to its neighboring tone both in the theme and in the variations, is delivered over to the right hand for the descent in the two concluding chords—through *eb* to *db*. This produces a forceful, definitive descent of the line, which was traced out within the tonic degree by the eighth notes in the fourth and fifth bars from the end. (See chapter 3, section 2, "The Third Progression.")

The old Breitkopf edition retained this notation, which is found in both autographs. The editor of the *Gesamtausgabe* struck it from the engraver's draft. Thus, once again, a beautiful refinement was lost. And wouldn't the performance of the piece be enhanced if the hand were so optically reminded of this descending line?

Beethoven's manner of writing in the third variation of the Sonata in Ab, op. 26, captures the sense of the voice leading in the most profound and brilliant way (see chapter 3, section, 5, "Ascending and Descending Register Transfers"):

Example 229.   Beethoven, Sonata in Ab Major, op. 26

The *bbb* of bar 4 is continued in the next bar as an inner voice, while the *db* of the bass is led to *c* of the upper voice. Beethoven places this *c* in the upper staff (note also the *cresc.*). To clarify the voice exchange, the left hand takes over the *bbb* and adds the third *eb–gb* to it. The same procedure is used at the repetition in bar 13, where the lower octave moves at the tone *c* for the first time into the right-hand staff. All conventional editions including the *Gesamtausgabe* (excepting Schenker's, published by Universal Edition) present the entire motion of the right hand in the upper staff; this places before the eye a false melodic line that moves across the leap at the beginning of bar 5.

In considering cases like these, one may after all become convinced that the issue is not merely one of philological trivialities—except perhaps such as have lain close to the heart of our great masters. Perhaps it would suffice if we, too, were to accord them the necessary reverence.[2] Only we ourselves could profit by doing so. As we consider such masterly ways of writing, Beethoven's remark in a letter to Ferdinand Ries (of December 20, 1822) takes on a deeper level of meaning: "For Beethoven, thank God, can write; of all else, indeed, he is incapable."[3]

---

2. Brahms took the greatest care in correcting, in his pocket score of the Haydn String Quartets op. 20, the deviations from the autograph in his possession. (Both score and autograph are now in the collection of the Gesellschaft der Musikfreunde, Vienna.)

[3. Translation by J. S. Shedlock, in *Beethoven's Letters: A Critical Edition with Explanatory Notes*, ed. A. C. Kalischer, trans. with preface by J. S. Shedlock (rpt. Freeport, N.Y.: Books for Libraries Press, 1969), II, p. 213.]

Appendix C

Supplementary Examples

Example 230. Supplement to Example 157

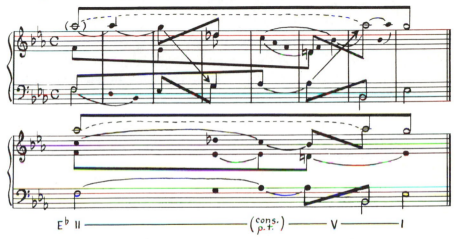

Example 231. Supplement to Example 160

Appendix D

Works of Heinrich Schenker[1]

The following is a list of Schenker's major publications, both in the original German as well as in English editions and translations. The German publications marked with an asterisk are in print.

Ein Beitrag zur Ornamentik. Vienna: Universal Edition, 1904.
    *New and enlarged edition, 1908. (See also under English translations.)
Neue musikalische Theorien und Phantasien.
    Vol. I: *Harmonielehre.* Stuttgart: Cotta, 1906. (See also under English translations.)
    Vol. II, Part I: *Kontrapunkt I.* Vienna: Universal Edition, 1910.
            Part II: *Kontrapunkt II.* Vienna: Universal Edition, 1922.
    Vol. III: *Der freie Satz.* Vienna: Universal Edition, 1935. *Second edition, edited and revised by Oswald Jonas. Vienna: Universal Edition, 1956. (See also under English translations.)
J. S. Bach. *Chromatische Phantasie und Fuge, Erläuterungsausgabe.* Vienna: Universal Edition, 1909. *Newly revised edition by Oswald Jonas. Vienna: Universal Edition, 1970.
Beethovens neunte Sinfonie. Vienna: Universal Edition, 1912.
Erläuterungsausgabe der letzten fünf Sonaten Beethovens. Vienna: Universal Edition.
    Op. 109, published 1913.
    Op. 110, published 1914.
    Op. 111, published 1915.

---

[1] A complete, comprehensive, carefully annotated list of Schenker's writings is to be found in David Beach, "A Schenker Bibliography" (*Journal of Music Theory 3*, no. 1 [1969]: 2–26; a revised edition has been published in *Readings in Schenker Analysis*, ed. Maury Yeston [New Haven: Yale University Press, 1977]). This bibliography also includes the most important books, monographs, and articles by other authors.

Op. 101, published 1920.

(Op. 106 was never published.)

*New edition of Op. 101, 109, 110, 111, revised by Oswald Jonas. Vienna: Universal Edition, 1970–71.

Der Tonwille, 10 issues. Vienna: A. Gutmann Verlag, 1921–24.

* Beethovens fünfte Sinfonie (reprinted from *Der Tonwille*). Vienna: Universal Edition. (See also under English translations.)

Das Meisterwerk in der Musik. Munich: Drei Masken Verlag.

Jahrbuch I, published 1925.

Jahrbuch II, published 1926.

Jahrbuch III, published 1930.

*Photographic reprint in one volume. Hildesheim: Georg Olms Verlag, 1974. (See also under English translations.)

Fünf Urlinie-Tafeln. New York: David Mannes School, and Vienna: Universal Edition, 1932. (See also under English editions.)

* Brahms, Oktaven und Quinten. Vienna: Universal Edition, 1934. (See also under English editions.)

Editions of Music

* Ph. Em. Bach, Klavierwerke (selections). Vienna: Universal Edition, 1902.

Beethoven, Klaviersonaten: Nach den Autographen und Erstdrucken rekonstruiert von Heinrich Schenker. Vienna: Universal Edition, 1921–23.

*New edition, revised by Erwin Ratz. Vienna: Universal Edition, 1947. (See also under English editions.)

Beethoven, Sonata op. 27 no. 2. Facsimile, with an introduction by Schenker. Vienna: Universal Edition, 1921.

English Editions and Translations

"J. S. Bach, The Largo from Sonata No. 3 for Unaccompanied Violin" (from *Das Meisterwerk in der Musik*, vol. 1). Translated by John Rothgeb. In *The Music Forum*, vol. 4. New York: Columbia University Press, 1976.

"J. S. Bach, The Sarabande of Suite No. 3 for Unaccompanied Violoncello" (from *Das Meisterwerk in der Musik*, vol. 2). Translated by Hedi Siegel. In *The Music Forum*, vol. 2. New York: Columbia University Press, 1970.

Beethoven, Complete Piano Sonatas. Reprint of the edition of 1921–23, with an introduction by Carl Schachter. New York: Dover, 1975.

"Beethoven, Fifth Symphony, First Movement." Translated by Elliott Forbes. In *Beethoven, Fifth Symphony* (Norton Critical Scores). New York: Norton, 1971.

"Brahms, Octaves and Fifths." Translated and annotated by Paul Mast. In *The Music Forum*, vol. 5. New York: Columbia University Press, 1979.

"A Contribution to the Study of Ornamentation." Translated by Hedi Siegel. In *The Music Forum*, vol. 4. New York: Columbia University Press, 1976.

Five Graphic Music Analyses. Photographic reprint of *Fünf Urlinie-Tafeln*, with an introduction by Felix Salzer. New York: Dover, 1969.

Free Composition. Translated and edited by Ernst Oster. New York: Longman Inc., 1979.

Harmony. Edited and annotated by Oswald Jonas. Translated by Elisabeth Mann Borgese. Chicago: University of Chicago Press, 1954; (paperback edition) Boston: M.I.T. Press, 1973.

"Organic Structure in Sonata Form" (from *Das Meisterwerk in der Musik,* vol. 2). Translated by Orin Grossman. *Journal of Music Theory* (1968). Reprinted in *Readings in Schenker Analysis,* ed. Maury Yeston, New Haven: Yale University Press, 1977.

Appendix E

List of Figures (Works Arranged
by Composer)

About the Translator

John Rothgeb first became acquainted with Heinrich Schenker's work—specifically, with *Harmony*—as an undergraduate student at Northwestern University in the early 1960s. On the recommendation of James Hopkins, his composition teacher and an alumnus of the Yale School of Music, he applied and was accepted for graduate study at that institution. This enabled him to pursue the study of Schenker's ideas in a more formal way under the guidance of Allen Forte. His studies at Yale led to an M.Mus. degree and subsequently to the Ph.D. in music theory.

In 1965 he began private study with the late Ernst Oster, the translator and editor of Schenker's *Free Composition* and a leading authority on the interpretation and application of Schenker's theory. He maintained close contact with Oster until the latter's death in 1977.

Rothgeb first met Oswald Jonas in 1969. During the years that followed, up until Jonas's death in 1978, he spent many illuminating hours with Jonas discussing music and music theory.

Articles, reviews, and translations by Rothgeb have been published in *Journal of Music Theory, Music Theory Spectrum,* and *The Music Forum,* among others. An anthology of Schenker's writings in translation, and a complete translation of Schenker's *Kontrapunkt,* are projected for the future. Rothgeb is currently Associate Professor of Music at State University of New York, Binghamton.